Spirituality
for the
21st Century

Experiencing God
in the
Catholic Tradition

A Symposium With Dr. Colleen M. Griffith,
Msgr. John J. Strynkowski, Rev. Michael J. Buckley, S.J.,
Sr. Mary Ann Hinsdale, I.H.M.,
Rev. Michael J. Himes, Rev. Kenan B. Osborne, O.F.M.

Edited by Dr. Richard W. Miller II

Liguori

LIGUORI, MISSOURI

Imprimi Potest:
Thomas F. Picton, C.Ss.R.
Provincial, Denver Province
The Redemptorists

ISBN 0-7648–1385-4
Library of Congress Catalog Card Number: 2006920287
© 2006, Catholic Community Foundation of Kansas City
Printed in the United States of America
10 09 08 07 06   5 4 3 2 1

Scripture quotations are from the *New Revised Standard Version of the Bible,* © 1989 by the Division of Christian Education of the National Council of Churches of Christ in the USA. Used with permission. All rights reserved.

Excerpt from *The Spiritual Exercises of St. Ignatius of Loyola* by Louis J. Puhl, S. J. (Newman Press 1951). Reprinted with permission of Loyola Press. To order copies of this book, call 1-800-621-1008 or visit *www.loyolabooks.org.*

To order, call 1-800-325-9521
www.liguori.org

Contents

Introduction

Dr. Richard W. Miller II, Assistant Professor of Systematic Theology, Creighton University

When asked by pollsters about their spiritual beliefs and practices, an overwhelming number of Americans respond that they both believe in God and regularly pray to God. Yet, they understand their spirituality to be a private affair, uninformed by religious institutions. They consider themselves spiritual but not religious. In his influential work *After Heaven: Spirituality in America Since the 1950s*, the distinguished sociologist of religion Robert Wuthnow assesses the present religious climate:

> *To be sure, the character of spirituality appears to be changing. Despite evidence that churches and synagogues are, on the surface, faring well, the deeper meaning of spirituality seems to be moving in a new direction in response to changes in U.S. culture. Indeed, the foundations of religious traditions seem to be less secure than in the past. Insisting that old phrases are cant, many Americans struggle to invent new languages to describe their faith. As they do, their beliefs are becoming more eclectic, and their commitments are often becoming more private.[1]*

Among the vast array of cultural factors that underlie this change, perhaps one is that religious traditions have failed to consistently

---

1. Robert Wuthnow, *After Heaven: Spirituality in America Since the 1950s* (Berkeley, California: University of California Press, 2000), 2.

make clear the connection between their doctrine and the spiritual lives of the members of their community.

This conference hopes to show the connection between the central mysteries of the Catholic faith and spirituality. This is not to impose from the outside an artificial theoretical structure on the interior life of the person. The dogmas of the faith are not and never have been abstract speculations disconnected from human experience. If God communicates himself in the innermost depths of the person, then there must be an intrinsic connection between the person's experience and the content of Christian dogmas. Indeed, the central dogmas of the Church came out of the Christian communities' experience of God's salvific activity through Jesus Christ by the power of the Holy Spirit. The definitive abstract articulation of the truth of their experience was worked out over the first seven centuries of the Church's life (ending with the Third Council of Constantinople 680-681) in the form of the doctrines of the Trinity and the Incarnation, the implications of which have been developed right through Vatican II in doctrinal statements on the human creature, redemption, and Eucharist. Consequently, in turning to the central mysteries of the faith to shed light on our spiritual lives we are not depersonalizing our interior lives, but we are reflecting anew upon the incomprehensible truth that the infinite God, the creator and sustainer of this vast universe, calls each and every one of us to the deepest most intimate friendship with him and each other so that we may share in the fullness of his life.

While elucidating that the connection between one's spirituality and the central dogmas and doctrines of the faith is not an imposition of an abstract theoretical structure upon the interior life of the person, it must also be made clear that this connection is not a heavy-handed attempt to prescribe a monolithic spirituality. For, as will become clear, there is not—and there never has been—a single Catholic spirituality; rather, there have been numerous spiritualities that have flourished within the Catholic tradition. Throughout the history of the Christian community, different religious thinkers took as central to their spiritualities different aspects of God's salvific activity. God as the infinite source of all goodness can be approached in countless ways. Thus, the symbols, images, or events around which any Christian spirituality is formed, while being true, do not exhaust the ways to God.

There is another reason for the reality of the multitude of spiritualities that speaks to the present situation as Robert Wuthnow describes it. If we take seriously God's will to save all human beings, then God is present to individuals, in all their uniqueness, drawing them by the Spirit through Christ to the Father, whether or not they are explicitly aware of God's influence in their lives. In addition, if we recognize that God calls the whole person to freely decide to accept or reject the influence of God in his or her life, then it is correct to maintain, as Pope Benedict XVI has suggested, that there are as many ways to God as there are men and women.[2]

To reflect on the meaning and significance of the central mysteries of the faith for spirituality is not to depersonalize the spiritual life or to restrict individuals to a single way to God but a guide and help in their unique path to God.

Let me leave you with the words of the great American Catholic novelist Flannery O'Connor:

> *For me a dogma is only a gateway to contemplation and is an instrument of freedom and not of restriction. It preserves mystery for the human mind.*[3]

---

2. Joseph Cardinal Ratzinger, *Salt of the Earth: The Church at the End of the Millennium: An Interview with Peter Seewald* (San Francisco, California: Ignatius Press, 1997), 32.

3. Flannery O'Connor, "Letter to A., 2 August, 1955" in *Collected Works,* ed. Sally Fitzgerald, The Library of America, 39 (New York: Literary Classics of the United States, 1988), 943.

1. What Is Spirituality?

Dr. Colleen M. Griffith, Institute for Religious Education and Pastoral Ministry, Boston College

In recent decades, "spirituality" has jumped to high-profile status, becoming a buzzword in our cultural milieu. Replete with positive connotations and strong valuations, it has emerged as a term serving many functions. It has acquired a reputation for being a cherished term of endearment, a safe haven for persons fed up with institutional religion, a medically approved stress-buster, and a welcome alternative for those bothered by exclusivist claims of their tradition of origin.

Given this variety of claims, one wonders what is spirituality, *really?* Is it primarily a reference to what makes us feel better and invites self-improvement, something that provides a safe haven, and/or is beneficial to our health? Is choosing "a spirituality" a matter of selecting a set of practices that suits our individual temperaments and hold potential for orienting our lives? Are spirituality and religion really separate paths, as many seem to suggest?

Despite the high esteem in which spirituality is held, there is much confusion apparent regarding its nature and function, many problematic assumptions and misconceptions riding on its coat tails. The "a.m. hours" of the twenty-first century will be critical for both "spirituality" and "religion," and the ensuing relationship between them. Will the new day usher in a more honest facing of the growing chasm between these two, or will it serve only to widen it? What are helpful ways of addressing this rift?

The question seems existentially pressing for "a people adrift,"[1]

---

1. This term arises from the title of a popular book written by Peter Steinfels. See *A People Adrift: The Crisis of the Roman Catholic Church in America* (New York: Simon and Schuster, 2003).

which is how many people today perceive themselves. Radically sensitized to the atrocities of our age, we harbor altered perspectives on nature and history in light of Auschwitz, 9/11, the Iraq War, terrorism, earthquakes, tsunamis. Our thinking about the present necessarily includes thoughts about those silenced, victimized, wiped out. Heightened consciousness has left us less naïve, more insecure, deeply saddened, and longing for insight while looking to our religious traditions for it.

Our Christian churches, in the meantime—institutions that have been carriers of rich tradition and beacons of light for many—have been showing their feet of clay in painful fashion, underscoring the human capacity for sinfulness and reckless bias. Whole communities have been rocked by sex abuse scandals, failures of accountability, absence of dialogue, signs of corruption, and abuses of power. Community members feel outraged and disillusioned; people struggle to maintain their footage, to hang on.

Speaking from the culturally specific standpoint of being North Americans in the twenty-first century, then, many of us find ourselves unhappily prone to what Ronald Rolheiser has described as the "triple crown" of "narcissism, pragmatism, and unbridled restlessness."[2] We have been conditioned to presume that life is all about us, and we have come to recognize this conditioning and its corresponding myth of autonomy. We have been taught well to value what will be fastest and most efficient without considering costs, and we have been applauded for grasping insatiably at the prospect of more experience for the mere sake of ever more experience. The result has been widespread dissatisfaction of heart. More and more people are deciding that the "triple crown" of narcissism, pragmatism, and unbridled restlessness is bankrupt. We're just plain tired of being frenetic, hassled, and agitated. Having a tough time centering, we feel

---

2. Ronald Rolheiser, *The Shattered Lantern: Rediscovering a Felt Presence of God*, 2nd ed. (New York: Crossroad, 2004), 27.

fragmented and are looking for something else. "Spirituality" holds strong attraction on all fronts.

The Spiritual Quest

In pursuit of something deeper, people find no shortage of resources that carry the name "spiritual practice" to draw upon. There has been an explosion of materials on spirituality in the last decade. In the preface to the anthology *Minding the Spirit: The Study of Christian Spirituality*, Elizabeth Dreyer and Mark Burrows comment: "A cursory glance at spirituality offerings in bookstores and on the World Wide Web quickly reveals the vastness and diversity of spiritualities and opportunities for spiritual pilgrims of every stripe."[3] The breadth of religious experiences being represented is truly remarkable. Also noteworthy, however, is the troubling fact that "spirituality" has become a financially astute investment, a reliable growth industry in corporate America. The task of sifting through the maze of what counts as authentic spirituality and what does not becomes a serious challenge.

Where does one begin to look when trying to decide about spiritual practices? How does one sort through bestsellers like *The Celestine Prophecy*, *Embraced by the Light*, and *Care of the Soul* that get placed on the same bookshelves in our bookstores as Augustine's *Confessions*, Teresa of Avila's *Interior Castle*, and *The Cloud of Unknowing*? How confusing it is to step up to what has been described as the "buffet table" of spirituality[4] to find a smorgasbord that includes traditional practices of prayer and ways of discernment alongside of practices associated with the occult, natural healing medicine, herbs and aromatherapy, new age crystals, Tai Chi, acupuncture, appearances of the Virgin Mary, secular retreats for business and

---

3. Elizabeth A. Dreyer and Mark S. Burrows, eds., *Minding the Spirit: The Study of Christian Spirituality* (Baltimore: John Hopkins University Press, 2005), xi.

4. See Michael Downey, *Understanding Christian Spirituality* (New York: Paulist Press, 1997), 5-29.

corporation executives, Progoff's intensive journal method, dream work, deep breathing, tantric sex, astrology, twelve-step programs, guided imagery, creative visualization, the Enneagram, Native American sweat lodges, and notably, in recent years, anything at all Celtic!

Are there criteria of adjudication that can help us to comb through everything that receives the name "spiritual practice"? How did the spirituality buffet table get this vast in the first place? Are there issues at stake in spirituality's universal popularity and endless possibilities? Should we be excited about the cultural space that spirituality is allotted in the twenty-first century or suspicious of it? The questions multiply.

The unmistakable surge of interest in spirituality in our time is in many ways welcome news. Spirituality highlights something very basic about being human. Sandra Schneiders describes it as "the capacity of persons to transcend themselves through knowledge and love, that is, to reach beyond themselves in relationship to others, and thus become more than self-enclosed material monads."[5] And spirituality emphasizes the need for practice; the role of practice in a religious tradition is vital if that tradition is to flourish. Spirituality demands engagement, intentionality, involvement, and these are hallmarks of an adult faith. It is inclusive of the body, of feeling and emotion, and as such, a breath of mountain air alongside of too much hardened rationalism. Spirituality serves as a helpful corrective to the narrowness, fundamentalism, and dogmatism to which our institutions sometimes fall prey. It can be a powerful egalitarian leveler in the face of clericalism, triumphalism, and hierarchicalism.

But there is also a downside evident in spirituality's swell in popularity. In their book *Selling Spirituality: The Silent Takeover of Religion*, Jeremy Carrette and Richard King examine "the commer-

---

5. Sandra M. Schneiders, "Religion vs. Spirituality: A Contemporary Conundrum," *Spiritus* 3.2 (Fall 2003):165.

cialization of 'religion' in the popular notion of spirituality."[6] Religion, sadly, is being "rebranded" as "spirituality." "Spirituality" is becoming the latest successful capitalist venture, a hot commodity that stimulates people at the level of desire.

Much of what is being sold today as radical and trendy spirituality is unmistakably privatized, accommodationist, and status quo. Carrette and King note: "In a sense, the most troubling aspect of many modern spiritualities is precisely that they are not troubling enough."[7] The socially transformative and prophetic aspects of the world's great religious traditions are being short-shrifted, while the retail values of accommodationist spiritualities get considered. One has only to observe the way that the business world has used the positive sheen of spirituality to promote its corporate interests to catch sight of "religion" being watered down and repackaged for consumption via "spirituality."[8]

In a culture lured by quick fixes and trendy appearances, accommodationist spiritualities carry appeal.[9] What ought to give us serious reasons for pause here are the individualist and corporatist uses of the term "spirituality," the promotion of consumerist, capitalist values under the auspices of "spirituality," and, most especially, the presentation of spirituality as the new replacement for religion.

Spirituality and Religion: Divorce or Life-giving Union?

Walking across any college campus these days one will hear some form of the persistent refrain: "I'm spiritual but not religious." This utterance signals something more than complacency in the face of

---

6. Jeremy Carrette and Richard King, *Selling Spirituality: The Silent Takeover of Religion* (London: Routledge, 2004), x.

7. Ibid., 5.

8. Ibid., 171.

9. Accomodationist spiritualities are often reflective of our proneness to narcissism, pragmatism, and frenetic restlessness.

or indifference to one's religious tradition of origin. It points to dissatisfaction and disaffiliation that often are the result of poor experiences of the institutionalization of religion. Absolutist rejection of religion on this basis is always unfortunate because, as Sandra Schneiders notes, it suggests "a failure to distinguish between the authentic and life-giving religious tradition and the spirituality to which it gives rise on the one hand, and its institutional form on the other."[10] This kind of totalizing rejection is, in Schneiders's words, "a classic case of curing a headache by decapitation."[11] Schneiders's point is well taken, yet the fact remains that institutions prone to corruption, hypocrisy, and abuses of power are more than mere headaches. Outright rejection of one's religious tradition on the basis of problematic encounters with religious institutions well may be akin to "throwing the baby out with the bath water," but it is time to demand that our institutions engage in more thoroughgoing self-reflection, honest critique, and necessary reform.

Our present situation is one in which spirituality is in ascendance while formal institutional participation in religion is on the decline.[12] Rightly or wrongly, people have come to think about spirituality in glowing terms, to associate it with personal and active agency and choice, to view it as an inclusive and transreligious word. Rightly or wrongly, persons have come to cast the word "religion" negatively, associating it with establishment institutions, hardened ideologies, and a certain stayedness.[13] "Spirituality" remains a thick signifier, able to hold multiple meanings and generate positive reception.

---

10. Schneiders, "Religion vs. Spirituality: A Contemporary Conundrum," 171.

11. Ibid.

12. Schneiders comments, "The irony of this situation evokes puzzlement and anxiety in the religious establishment, scrutiny among theologians, and justification among those who have traded the religion of their past for the spirituality of their present" ("Religion vs. Spirituality: A Contemporary Conundrum," 163).

13. See Sandra Schneiders, "Religion and Spirituality: Strangers, Rivals, or Partners?," *The Santa Clara Lectures* 6.2 (February, 2000)

"Religion" continues to struggle to escape its reduction to flawed institutional expressions that cast it in a poor light.

The split between "spirituality" and "religion" shows few signs of redress despite the deleterious effects that it has on each. Religion that is bereft of spirituality becomes anemic, irrelevant, and self-serving. Spirituality that lacks connection with religious tradition has no roots, lacking both community and tradition. It has no recourse to the benefits of a larger body of discourse and accountability and is prone to hyperbole and instability.

The task of addressing the gulf between spirituality and religion becomes one of utmost importance for us all. The collection of writings of which this essay is a part represents one attempt to respond to this chasm, all the while construing "religion" as inclusive of, and wider than, religious institutions. One specific way of diminishing the separation between spirituality and religion—the latter understood in broader terms—is to explore carefully and intentionally the connection between spirituality and the doctrines of one's specific faith.

Spirituality and Doctrine in the Christian Tradition

In Christian terms, the word "spirituality" can be traced to the letters of Paul where he uses the Greek term *pneuma* to signal a life lived in harmony with God's spirit. Spirituality implies a capacity to live in alignment with the Spirit of God, an ability to commit oneself to a set of consciously chosen practices that foster Christian discipleship. Philip Sheldrake offers the following definition of a distinctively *Christian spirituality*: "...[S]pirituality is the whole of human life viewed in terms of a conscious relationship with God, in Jesus Christ, through the indwelling of the Spirit, and within the community of believers."[14]

Sheldrake's definition is a particularly apt one as it highlights a Christian conception of God and an understanding of the human

---

14. Philip Sheldrake, *Spirituality and Theology: Christian Living and the Doctrine of God* (Maryknoll, New York: Orbis, 1998), 35.

both in relationship with Christ and with respect to a larger community. This definition relies heavily upon Christian doctrine in its Trinitarian, anthropological, Christological, and ecclesial references. But a majority of persons who identify themselves as Christian assume that spirituality and doctrine are separate and distinct entities with little in common.

Ironically, doctrines serve as benchmarks of the spiritual wisdom of the Christian community over time. They provide Christians with a worldview by which they can better understand themselves, their relationship to God, Christ, others and the world. Doctrines are normative beliefs that are expressive of the Christian community's central insights regarding the mystery of Christ. As a response to the mystery of God in Christ, no single doctrine, or all of them cumulatively, ever exhausts the reality of that mystery. No doctrine makes claims to do so.

The primary purpose of doctrine is to be evocative, to nurture the Christian community's relationship to Christ. In his book *By What Authority?*, Richard Gaillardetz reminds us of this: "The earliest instance of church dogma or doctrine of any kind was found in the ancient creeds produced by the early Church. These creeds were initially developed for use in sacramental initiation and worship. We tend to miss this because of changes in the way that we understand the verb 'to believe.'"[15] The Greek word *pisteuo*, and in similar fashion the Latin verb *credo*, imply making a promise in light of a personal and committed relationship with God. Although the primary intent of Christian doctrine, as evidenced in the early Church, is to serve a relational way of life (rather than to communicate mere knowledge) many contemporary Christians do not operate with this sense of doctrine. Most assume that doctrines are juridical and legislative propositions written by a magisterial elite to which they must give assent. Few understand the connection between doctrine and

---

15. Richard R. Gaillardetz, *By What Authority?* (Collegeville: Liturgical Press, 2003), 93.

spirituality, because that specific connection has not been made explicit enough, and it has not always been valued sufficiently.

So what does fostering a closer connection between doctrine and spirituality entail? I propose four points:

1. There needs to be a bringing together of all that has been associated with both theory and practice. Ever since the Enlightenment divided theoretical and practical reason, we have labored with a false dichotomy with respect to theory and practice. The epistemic privileging of normative claims (as found in doctrines) over actual practice (as found in spiritualities lived in the humdrums of everyday lives) is less likely to occur when theory and practice are viewed as inextricably bound, interlocked, and not to be split in order to be hierarchically ordered later. Any continued claims for clear and distinct demarcation between theory and practice are singularly unhelpful. It is time for practice to assume a place of more dignity in all of this, to be seen as more than the mere application point for doctrine.

2. There must be more honest recognition, particularly by the magisterium, that formulations of Christian facts have value insofar as persons and communities appropriate them and imbue them with value. A genuine understanding and holding of doctrine involves more than an ability to recite its claims, more than a grasp of its intellectual content. Real understanding implies conscious appropriation that is enlivening for and transformative of the individuals themselves. Lived faith cannot be reduced to a set of cognitive beliefs and the memorization of those beliefs. Knowledge alone will not suffice, and it should ✓ not. A genuine grasp of doctrine entails a willingness and ability to embody the wisdom inherent in that doctrine. This calls for levels of appropriation that will influence dispositions and invite practices, all the while providing a deeper life of faith for individuals themselves and for communities of faith.

3.   Nurturing more connection between spirituality and doctrine in the lives of contemporary Christians will demand more direct acknowledgment that our spiritualities are only the richer when we draw upon central components of the Christian community's self-understanding, as expressed in doctrine, in order to live creatively and well. We cannot speak about Christian spirituality today in singular terms; it is more accurate to note the spiritualities of Christians, as demonstrated throughout history.[16] There is certainly commonality in the various expressions of Christian spirituality, but individuals and specific communities still have to discern their particular paths, ways of prayer, and modes of praxis. Those persons with the clearest and fullest sense of the content of their religious tradition are ever the ones most able to imagine rich practices and meaningful ways of embodying their tradition.

4.   Spirituality's contribution to what has been called "the noetic content of the tradition" needs deliberate underscoring. Just as doctrine informs spirituality, spirituality informs doctrine. Spirituality cannot be the "mug" for the "jug" of doctrine. Its vision spills wider. Sandra Schneiders writes:

> *One has only to think of the teaching of John of the Cross about the equality of the soul with God, Julian of Norwich's insight into the femininity of Jesus, or Teresa of Avila's conviction about the role of the humanity of Jesus in mystical experience, to realize that spirituality is not simply the application in practice of the teachings of theology....*[17]

---

16. See Philip Sheldrake, *Spirituality and History* (Maryknoll, New York: Orbis, 1995).

17. Sandra Schneiders, "A Hermeneutical Approach to the Study of Spirituality," in *Minding the Spirit*, eds. Elizabeth A. Dreyer and Mark S. Burrows (Baltimore: John Hopkins University Press, 2005), 54.

The spiritualities of persons, their practices of lived faith, can and should contribute to the noetic content of the Christian tradition. To say anything less is to suggest that tradition is some kind of finished monument rather than a work in progress. Lawrence Cunningham offers the following:

> *The historical tradition of Christianity, shaped by creed, ethos, and worship, is both circumscribed and elastic. It has a definite shape, but it is a shape that is in process and not finished. There is no Golden Age when a synthetic harmony existed, and there will be none short of the eschaton. The great tradition is, and should be, polyphonic. The tradition, in short, is complex and it learns.[18]*

The spiritualities of persons have much to contribute to the Church's traditioning process,[19] but this is seldom spoken about.

These are four strategies meant to be starting points, suggestive guidelines that can yield more fluency with respect to Christian faith, not just minimal literacy. If we place a stronger accent on the linkage between spirituality and doctrine, people will be more inclined to learn the doctrines of their tradition, since knowing them will have less to do with orthodoxy checklists, and more to do with the chance to learn their wisdom for life. A change becomes apparent here, a shift from having a general grasp of one's tradition to being grasped by it.

In doctrines that are radically spiritual and spiritualities that are richly doctrinal, we are renewed, less likely to carry our faith in the mind alone, and more likely to engage it in lively fashion.

18. Lawrence S. Cunningham, "Extra Arcam Noe: Criteria for Christian Spirituality," in *Minding the Spirit*, eds. Elizabeth A. Dreyer and Mark S. Burrows (Baltimore: John Hopkins University Press, 2005), 175.

19. For an excellent discussion of the traditioning process, see Terrence Tilley, *Inventing Catholic Tradition* (Maryknoll, New York: Orbis, 2000).

In conclusion, what can be said about a Christian spirituality? It is a spirituality suffused by doctrine and yet, as religious experience, it spills beyond the confines of doctrine. It presumes the human capacity for relational life with God in Christ, made possible by God's own initiative and human receiving of God's self-giving. And it is communal through and through.

A Christian spirituality entails a commitment to a lived faith, a faith that acts, one that matures and deepens as we move to more expansive and inclusive ways of thinking and loving. It is nurtured by consciously chosen practices that foster transformation and conversion, enabling us to become more authentic and integrated selves in relation to God, others, and the created order. Finally, a Christian spirituality is forever connected to the personhood, story, and vision[20] of Jesus Christ, seeking to reenact that story and embody that vision in all of the ways of which human beings are capable. Christian spirituality is anything but a narrow faith argued in the mind alone.

---

20. In my use of the language of "story and vision," I am indebted to the work of Thomas Groome. See Groome, *Sharing Faith: A Comprehensive Approach to Religious Education and Pastoral Ministry* (San Francisco: Harper, 1991).

2. Spirituality and the Triune God

Msgr. John J. Strynkowski, Former Executive Director of the Secretariat for Doctrine and Pastoral Practices, U.S.C.C.B.

The massive outpouring of pilgrims to Rome upon the death of Pope John Paul II was certainly a sign of his ability to speak to the spirit of men and women today, especially the young. In the words of Cardinal Carlo Martini, former Archbishop of Milan, they saw in the late pope a spiritual father. Commenting further on this in a homily he gave recently on the occasion of the twenty-fifth anniversary of his episcopal ordination, Martini said: "Watching the people who were passing in front of the body of John Paul II, I thought that it would be of little value to venerate a spiritual father of humanity if God had not spoken in the intimate precincts of every heart, showing to each one of us what is our task, our vocation, what we should do, what is demanded of each one of us and not of another....God himself wants to enter into intimate communion with every human being as a guide through the discovery of his or her mission and vocation."[1]

The God who wants to enter into communion with every human being is, of course, the triune God. This is one of the doctrines of the Church that contributes to the distinctiveness of Christian spirituality. The triune God—Father, Son, and Holy Spirit—has taken hold of those who have been baptized in such a way that when we gather for liturgy we pray publicly to the Father, through the Son, in the Holy Spirit. But these divine persons have also made the intimate depths of our being their dwelling place. We are called to be attentive, indeed obedient, to their presence and direction. In this

---

1. My translation from the Italian text as it appears on the website of the Archdiocese of Milan.

essay, I concentrate on what the presence of the triune God means for us as Christians and for our spirituality. At the same time, I recognize that this same God is also present in every human being, where he seeks to drive each one of us to an ever-deepening recognition of his presence and guidance throughout life.

I begin, therefore, with a simple description of what it means to be human, show its triune structure, and then view it from the perspective of our Trinitarian faith. There have been many truly profound theological efforts to show a Trinitarian structure of human nature that images and actualizes the presence of the triune God within us. A review of that literature would require a substantial tome and take us beyond the purposes of this conference. I do not feign originality but am simply proposing a description of human nature that I hope is relevant for our time and for our Christian spirituality.

I suggest, therefore, the following formula: "I am searching for meaning." I think every human being at one time or another, if not constantly, will recognize that. And I believe that it is a statement that has a Trinitarian structure.

First of all, "I am." Our existence has to fill us with awe. That—after some thirteen billion years from the big bang, in a universe with countless numbers of stars, and on a planet with more than six billion other human beings—I exist is certainly a source of amazement. It is also a source of wonderment. Why do I exist? How is it that I live in this particular moment of human history and in this particular place? I am a searcher. And the search is relentless. I want to know and what I want to know is more than just the particularities of my family genealogy. The sciences, the arts, philosophy and theology can all contribute to my search. But I search for more than just origins and causes. I also want meaning for my life. That meaning can be of many different sorts. It can be a career, a profession, a cause, an idea. It can be money, power, or prestige. But the meaning that brings greatest satisfaction is personal relationships and my ability to do something for others—humanity in general, my nation, my local community, my friends, my family.

This is who we are. We are searching for meaning. We are. We search. We find meaning. To this triadic structure of our human nature corresponds the triune God of our Christian faith. "We believe in one God, the Father, the Almighty, maker of heaven and earth...." This is the first affirmation of the Creed we profess on Sundays. We believe that we come from God and are sustained in existence by God. At every moment of my existence, I am wanted, known, and loved by God. Nothing of me escapes or exceeds God's wanting me, knowing me, and loving me. God wants me more than I want myself, knows me better than I know myself, and loves me more than I love myself. I am because of God.

Augustine and Thomas Aquinas are quite different in their analysis of the intimacy that exists between the Creator and human beings. But our times could benefit significantly from what each of them offers. The drama of the conversation with God in Augustine's *Confessions* is a marvelous paradigm for the prayerful conversations to which every human being is called and from which every human being can draw sustenance. Thomas Aquinas's analogy of being—certainly more abstract than Augustine's sometimes anguished conversation—opens the door to a mysticism flowing from the awareness of the closeness of God as he calls us into existence and sustains us in existence.

Christian spirituality ought to awaken awe and wonderment at the mere fact that I am. Given the harshness of historical realities, all of us, like Job, might wish at times that we were not, that we had not seen the light of day. But fundamentally we remain struck by the fact of our being and even more by the mystery of our being. It is not simply Job-like suffering that raises the question of why we are. The very ecstasies of life raise the same question. Why we have been blessed is a mystery too. But there are other questions as well. Who am I? What is my role in this moment of history and in this spot on the earth? Where am I going? What do I mean? This last question translates as what do I really mean when I say something and what do I mean to others, to the unfolding of human history in my particular circumstances, and ultimately to myself?

Secondly, I search. As a Church we believe in the Holy Spirit. I want to propose that the Holy Spirit is the source of our searching. In the Scriptures the Holy Spirit pushes and drives people beyond themselves. Think of David, raised from being a shepherd boy to king of Israel after being anointed with oil and the Spirit. Think of the prophet Ezekiel, taken by the Spirit to preach in the desert to the dry and scattered bones. Think of the apostles, wind-blown by the Spirit at Pentecost to proclaim the Good News about Jesus Christ. The Holy Spirit leads people beyond themselves to achieve God's will and God's work. In the Scriptures, to use the images of Jean Daniélou, the Holy Spirit is a storm, a hurricane, forcing people out of comfortable environments and into new ventures.

As stated earlier, I suggest that we see the Holy Spirit as the source of our searching, our restlessness, until we find meaning. The Apostle Paul describes the Spirit's guidance in our confusion: "Likewise the Spirit helps us in our weakness; for we do not know how to pray as we ought, but that very Spirit intercedes with sighs too deep for words"(Romans 8:26). We do not know what we want, where we can find meaning. The Spirit works within us to lead us where we might not even want to go. "And God, who searches the heart, knows what is the mind of the Spirit, because the Spirit intercedes for the saints according to the will of God" (Romans 8:27). And what is God's will? In John's Gospel Jesus says: "When the Spirit of truth comes, he will guide you into all the truth; for he will not speak on his own, but will speak whatever he hears....He will glorify me, because he will take what is mine and declare it to you" (John 16:13-14). Like the wind that makes a tree bend in a certain direction, so too the Spirit leads us in a certain direction—to Jesus Christ, Word of God, ultimate meaning for us.

Thirdly, then, I find meaning. We believe that Jesus Christ is the Word—the Logos—that has become flesh. He is the Word that gives meaning to our lives. The lengthy discourses between Jesus and others in the Gospel of John describe dramatically how his hearers found meaning in him. In Jesus Christ we find the ultimate rationale, the ultimate logos, the ultimate meaning for our lives. It is not just an intellectual meaning—it is the meaning of one person for another, it is the meaning of mutuality, it is the meaning of indwelling. It is the meaning of a crucified and risen Lord, with all the hope, peace, and love that he brings.

I am searching for meaning. I come from the Father, made a restless searcher by the Holy Spirit, led by him to the Word made flesh, Jesus Christ, ultimate meaning for my existence. This triune God dwells within me. But am I attentive enough? Happily, God within us shakes us out of our indifference by his presence in the community of the Church. God is present in the saints. God is present in our brothers and sisters. God is present in the sacraments. God is present in those who teach and shepherd. We are truly surrounded by countless witnesses. A Christian spirituality must be Trinitarian and ecclesial. The Father, through the Son and in the Holy Spirit, reaches us through visible channels and leads us into ever-greater meaning for our lives.

The Church, the witness of holiness, liturgy, teaching, and governance all have their source in the Scriptures. A Trinitarian spirituality can be profoundly enriched by constant encounter with Scripture. What God wants to say within us should be guided by the divinely-inspired Scriptures. That is why it is so heartening to see the tradition of *lectio divina*—prayerful reflection on the Scriptures—being urged from so many quarters, including Pope John Paul II in the program he outlined for the third millennium in his Apostolic Letter *Novo Millennio Ineunte* (At the Beginning of the Third Millennium): "It is especially necessary that listening to the word of God should become a life-giving encounter, in the ancient and ever valid tradition of *lectio divina*, which draws from the biblical text the living word which questions, directs and shapes our lives."[2]

Out of such prayer should come a sense of mission. After all, we know the triune God through the mission of the Son and the Holy Spirit. That they were sent to us means that now we are sent to others. Any Christian spirituality—but especially a Trinitarian one—will demonstrate its validity by the extent to which it leads its followers *ad extra*, beyond the comfortable confines of the Christian community into the world. This world has sometimes been described as a desert and, if one looks only at the anxieties, confusion, injustices, and conflicts in the world—to the exclusion of the immense efforts by so many to ensure justice, peace, equality, prosperity, to the exclusion also of the sincere search for truth and community, and to the exclusion of the exercise of compassion and self-sacrifice for others, all of these being signs of God's presence and grace in the world—then to speak of some aspect of the world as a desert is justified. But that is where the Christian belongs because Christ was there, in the desert, before us. Christ, however, came out of the desert unsullied. For the Christian, faced with all the consequences of original sin, the struggle in the desert can be fraught with ambiguities. I am reminded of some words of Cardinal John Henry Newman in a sermon entitled *Sins of Infirmity*:

> *We have much to be forgiven; nay, we have the more to be forgiven the more we attempt. The higher our aim, the greater our risks. They who venture much with their talents, gain much, and in the end they hear the words, "Well done, good and faithful servant." But they have so many losses in trading by the way, that to themselves they seem to do nothing but fail. They cannot believe that they are making any progress; and*

---

2. John Paul II, *Novo Millennio Ineunte* (At the Beginning of the Third Millennium), in Origins 30:31 (2001): 501, no. 39.

though they do, yet surely they have much to be forgiven in
all their services. They are like David, men of blood; they
fight the good fight of faith, but they are polluted with the
contest.[3]

Awareness of the Trinity within us leads us to mission. But awareness of the Trinity within us means that we are willing to acknowl-
edge the closeness of God to us, his dwelling deep down at the core
of our being, his wanting us, knowing us, and loving us. And yet
there are obstacles to letting ourselves be so aware of God. These
obstacles are theological, cultural, and psychological.

First, the theological. What I intend here is people's inaccurate
theology. We are afflicted with incorrect images of God. If someone,
for example, has the image of God as vindictive, it is not likely that
he or she is willing to be engaged by God in intimate conversation.
Such an image of God is unnecessary today in light of all of the
exegetical work that has been done in recent decades to locate this
image with the particular context of Israel's early history and to show
how it was transcended within the Bible itself in later stages of biblical composition.

Another image hindering intimacy with God is that of God
dwelling in a distant heaven. If God is far away, communication is
quite difficult. But heaven is not some distant place, as was pointed
out by Pope John Paul II in an address in 1999: "[Heaven] is neither
an abstraction nor a physical place in the clouds, but a living, personal relationship with the Holy Trinity." He went on to encourage a
"personalist language" as "better suited to describing the state of
happiness and peace we will enjoy in our definitive communion with
God."[4] Such an approach is all the more necessary when we live in a
world which we understand to be the result of a long evolutionary

---

3. John Henry Newman, *Parochial and Plain Sermons* (San Francisco: Ignatius Press, 1987), 1086.

4. John Paul II, Address at General Audience of July 21, 1999.

process. There are many theologians today who offer wonderful insights into our understanding of God in the light of evolutionary theory, but this work needs to be more widely disseminated.

A third image that can hinder closeness to God is that of God as male. The *Catechism of the Catholic Church* offers a helpful corrective: "In no way is God in man's image. He is neither man nor woman. God is pure spirit in which there is no place for the difference between the sexes."[5] There is much catechesis needed here.

Second, there are also cultural obstacles to intimate conversation with God. We live in a culture that fosters countless distractions. There are sufficient analyses of this to exempt me from having to comment further. But I am reminded of a quotation from Erich Fromm that I read many years ago: "Theologians and philosophers have been saying for a century that God is dead, but what we must confront now is the possibility that man is dead, transformed into a thing, a producer, a consumer, an idolater of other things."[6] In the face of these at-times-overwhelming distractions it becomes all the more urgent for us to foster community within our parishes—especially by the promotion of small communities—where common prayer and reflection are possible, thus nourishing individual prayer and reflection. This effort at community building is also a consequence of Trinitarian spirituality—divine relationships mirrored in human relationships.

Another phenomenon of our culture, though not particular to our culture, is the fascination with stories. People seek meaning in stories. As Cardinal Newman pointed out long ago, hearts are moved, not by syllogisms, but by imagination. There are certain basic themes to be found in all stories (for example, fall and redemption, or the hard journey by which the innocent one learns

---

5. *Catechism of the Catholic Church*, 370.

6. As quoted in an article by David Poling in the *Saturday Review* of May 14, 1966, p. 52.

wisdom and compassion) that can be connected to the fundamental Christian narrative. We need to become more adept at making those connections.

Third, there can also be psychological obstacles to intimate communion with the triune God. Anxiety about intimacy is common. To admit that God knows us better than we know ourselves and that he wants to push us beyond our current boundaries may be more than we can accept at a given time. We need to remember the patience of God and, perhaps even more, God's humility. God sustains us but does not force us. I quote some helpful words from the Jesuit theologian John Wright:

> *The eternal God enters into a dialogue with his frail and sinful creatures. His action so transcends all the limitations of finite being that it penetrates the most intimate and personal of our acts, our free response to the divine invitation, causing all its perfection and actuality, yet leaving it truly our response, an act whose determination is ultimately our responsibility.*[7]

God entrusts to us an awesome responsibility to choose to be fully human or less so, to advance his will or to hinder it. Such entrustment by God should free us to be more attentive to his presence within us and to his voice through Scripture and the Church community. Contemporary theological work on God's humility and the relationship between divine providence and our freedom needs to be further disseminated so that we can be more transparent to the presence of the triune God.

I am searching for meaning. A Trinitarian spirituality means that my search is neither finished nor in vain. The God who created

---

7. John Wright, "Divine Knowledge and Human Freedom: the God who Dialogues," *Theological Studies* 38 (1977): 477.

me spurs me on to greater understanding and love, to ever-greater meaning for my life. And when I have reached the end of my life, I will know how much I was truly wanted by God, known by him, and loved by him.

3. Spirituality and the Incarnate God

Rev. Michael J. Buckley, S.J., Boston College

W e have been invited to explore the meaning and the religious significance of what has been called "incarnational spirituality," that is, a spirituality that takes its inspiration and its character from God Incarnate. This project obviously extends and differentiates our more general inquiry into spirituality, but herein also lies our initial problem.[1]

This problem is constituted by an unspoken presupposition that we all know and concur on what is meant by "spirituality," know enough, indeed, so that we can distinguish spiritualities into kinds and judge their effectiveness in giving some direction to our lives. This presupposition seems to me unwarranted. I suspect, on the contrary, that each of us probably operates from at least a somewhat different understanding of spirituality. If so, before speaking of incarnational spirituality, we ought to clarify both what is meant by "spirituality" in general and how it is being used here as we specify its character further. Let me do this somewhat schematically.

Prenote:

I. If you look carefully through the experiences and the long annals of the Church, you will find in all of its manifold subcommunities and associations major personal influences. Individual people embodied and radiated and taught either in the

---

1. Earlier drafts of statements and sections of this article have appeared in the following: "Jesuit Spirituality as a Stimulus to the Ecumenical Movement," *CIS* (Rome: Centrum Ignatianum Spiritualitatis, 1988). Paper delivered before the International Society of Jesuit Ecumenists, Summer 1987. Revised as: "'Always Growing in Devotion...': Jesuit Spirituality as a Stimulus to Ecumenical Involvement," published as *Chancellor's Address VI*, Regis College, Toronto, Canada, 1989.

practices of their life or in the groups that they fostered a *particular and characteristic religious pattern of living,* a pattern by which one could approach God or, better, be approached by God. That *pattern of commitments and practices and prayer* is what I would call a spirituality.

II. This pattern of life can also come to specify not only a single individual's relationship with God but also that of a religious community or a religious culture or a parish or a school or a circle of friends or a family. It can give these their peculiar religious features. Yes, even an individual family can possess its own religious character. And when this pattern of interaction with God—what John Dewey called "experience," whether personal or communal, whether great or small—is mediated by the reality that is Christ and inspired by his Spirit, we are talking about a Christian spirituality. But even further, while all Christian spiritualities have this in common that they derive their origins and their founding inspiration from Jesus Christ and his Spirit, still each will differ somewhat in the manner in which Christ's teaching is assimilated and his inspiration personalized. Hence, the massive pluralism among Christian spiritualities. Indeed, John of the Cross maintained that the closer one comes to God, the more individuated will be the spirituality in which he or she advances toward God. For God moves each person in his or her own way, "gradually bringing the soul *after its own manner* to the other end [which is] spiritual wisdom."[2]

III. From this initial understanding of "spirituality," I think that we can abstract at least *two coordinates* by which every Christian spirituality can be charted. We can talk about "God" and we can

---

2. John of the Cross, *The Ascent of Mount Carmel,* trans. Kieran Kavanaugh and Otilio Rodriguez, revisions by Kavanaugh (Washington, D.C.: Institute of Carmelite Studies, 1991). II. 17. #2-3, pp. 205-206.

talk about a human "pathway toward God"—that is, a characteristic mode of proceeding. Every distinct Christian spirituality will specify or determine how these figure within it and, as a consequence, spell out their own particular character.

A. First, and absolutely primary, is God, that is, [1] the manner in which the incomprehensible "God" is *specified* or *understood* or [2] the *images* by which the divine mystery is symbolized or [3] the *events* in which the divine presence is realized and by which it is principally marked. As Joseph Wall has pointed out, Christians as such will not have contradictory views of the divine reality.[3] But our finite human intelligence must select among the infinity that is God certain attributes and events as primary, as governing.

   1. John of the Cross, in the first book of the *Ascent of Mt. Carmel*, sees God primarily as the infinite one, demanding consequently a stark detachment from anything finite if one is to be united with him.

   2. In Meister Eckhart, God is understood as the One who is above being and whose omnipresence allows for a unity between spirituality, mysticism, and philosophical inquiry.

   3. Teresa of Avila characteristically refers to God as His Majesty while Dorothy Day finds God as the one whose compassion draws her to the kind of community reflected in *The Catholic Worker*.

B. Second, the other factor that will stamp or specify any spirituality is the manner, the events, the change, and the practices through which human beings are united with God so conceptualized or imaged. What does God (as understood

---

3. See Joseph B. Wall, S.J., *The Providence of God in the Letters of Saint Ignatius* (San Jose: Smith-McKay, 1958), 2. This discussion of the crucial role of the divine attributes in specifying a spirituality is greatly indebted to this monograph of Joseph Wall.

in this spirituality), call us to live out, ask us to become, encourage us to practice? Again there is much here that is common to all Christians, but there are also peculiar journeys, experiences, and histories that specialize divine grace for this person or for this community.

IV. This set of coordinates, then, allows us to ask two questions about any spirituality or, in this case, about incarnational spirituality:

A. What understanding or apprehension of God is dominant or strongly characteristic of this spirituality—while allowing for all sorts of variation?

B. What does God so understood draw from a human being as an appropriate manner of life? What will be the career or community or practices or life that will respond to God so understood? What is the manner in which human beings can be detached enough or occupied enough or prayerful enough to be drawn by grace towards unity with God imagined or experienced in this way?

Now, with these two questions in mind, let us look at what is incarnational spirituality: God and the manner of living that responds to God.

Part One: The Mystery of God

Paradoxically, it might be better to take that look by beginning with what incarnational spirituality is not.

One of the greatest and most influential works in Christian spirituality is Gregory of Nyssa's *Life of Moses*. Written sometime around 390, it presented Moses in the desert and Moses ascending Mt. Sinai as the example for a Christian spirituality. Among the factors that essentially formed this spirituality and permeated it is Moses' withdrawal from active involvement with "the affairs of men."[4] Moses lived alone in the Midian desert "away from the turmoil of the marketplace," while on Mt. Sinai the condition for his entering into the darkness of God was separation from the people. Before ascending that Mountain to find a new union with God, Moses must clean all of his garments because they represent "in a figure the outward respectability of life." They are the outward pursuits of life.[5] Animals are not to pasture on the Mountain for "in the contemplation of the intelligibles, we surpass the knowledge that originates with the senses."[6] Indeed we must go not only beyond all emotions, but beyond all concepts as well and "every opinion derived from some preconception."[7] Moses would eventually communicate to his people something of what he had learned about God in the experience of darkness and solitude, but Gregory of Nyssa never says that he learned about God from the people or the finite things he encountered.[8] All finite things must be transcended.

The reason behind this progressive and utter renunciation lies with Gregory's understanding of the mystery of God. He stated at the beginning of his *Life of Moses* that "we must take up the task that lies before us, taking God as the guide in our treatise.[9] And how is God fundamentally perceived? God is the infinite.[10] Thus, the metaphor of "the ascent" becomes of central importance for Gregory, leaving all finite things visible and invisible behind as one ascends into the darkness of the incomprehensible God—incomprehensible

4. Abraham J. Malherbe and Everett Ferguson, "Introduction," to Gregory of Nyssa, *The Life of Moses,* trans., introduction and notes by Abraham J. Malherbe and Everett Ferguson (New York: Paulist Press, 1978), 9-10.

5. *Moses*, #155, 92-93.

6. *Moses*, #156, 93.

7. *Moses*, #157, 93.

8. Malherbe and Ferguson, "Introduction," 10.

9. *Moses*, #3, 30.

10. Thus Malherbe and Ferguson can assert that for Gregory "the fundamental doctrine for his spirituality is the divine infinity" ("Introduction," 14).

because infinite. Indeed, not only does Gregory describe the Christian progress under this central metaphor of a laborious ascent of a mountain, but also he is "perhaps the first Christian author to do so."[11] It is a metaphor that will continue through the Fathers of the Church and into the great Spanish Renaissance mystics, reaching into Thomas Merton's *Seven Storey Mountain* and *The Ascent to Truth*. This is the "ascent tradition," and it demands renunciation of all finite things so that one can become like the formless, figureless pure actuality that is God. One ascends and leaves behind all things in order to become more and more "like God."

Now, so much of this is precisely what incarnational spirituality does not accentuate. And where these two kinds of spirituality perhaps differ most profoundly—differ, not contradict; complement, not repudiate, as I hope to point out—is the manner in which they apprehend the incomprehensible God. Ascent spirituality emphasizes God as utterly transcendent and above movement, change, form, or figure, often—like Gregory of Nyssa—taking infinity as the specifying divine attribute. Incarnational spirituality, on the other hand, takes God's involvement with the world and with human history as its focus, as the fundamental key to his loving nature. This involvement with human beings and the world of being human realizes itself in two ways: God's providential government of all things and the Incarnation—God's descent into matter and history, to become part of creation—as the event that most manifests this abiding providence. Thus, the theology that comes out of ascent spirituality asks: What is God? The theology that comes out of descent spirituality asks: What is God doing in the world? The first looks for God in the incomprehensibility, in the darkness that is beyond anything finite; the second, looks for God descending salvifically into everything that is finite.

---

11. Michael Cox, *A Handbook of Christian Mysticism* (London: The Aquarian Press, 1986), 70.

Ascent spirituality has framed the human response in Moses' ascent of Sinai. The various components of this ascent are to be analogized to the various stages of growth in detachment and contemplation. Incarnational or descent spirituality as in Irenaeus, Hopkins, Ignatius of Loyola, and Teilhard de Chardin has framed its image of the human response in a movement that is almost the reverse. The paradigm for that movement is the Incarnation and the abiding and dynamic providence of God: God entering into the world, indeed, God becoming part of this world, actually "working and laboring for me" in the world, as Ignatius found him, because he longs for the salvation of human beings.[12]

One can see this difference in the contemplation of the Trinity. Ascent spirituality tends to contemplate the Trinity in its own interior life; incarnational or descent spirituality tends to contemplate the Trinity in its self-communication in grace and through history. In the *Spiritual Exercises* of Saint Ignatius, for example, the exercitant is not called to contemplate the eternal spiration of the Spirit, but to "contemplate how the Three Divine Persons were looking down upon the whole flat or round of the whole world, full of human beings; and how, seeing that all were going to hell [to a definitive absence of God], it was decreed in their eternity that the Second Person should become man to save the human race. And so it was done."[13] This contemplation does not focus upon the eternal generation of the Word, but upon the Word's entering human life, upon the Incarnation.

This religious focus upon the reality that is the incarnate, providential God can seem almost the opposite of ascent mysticism. Incarnational spirituality is not to find God away from matter and the finite, images and concepts, human history, grace and sin, the

---

12. Ignatius of Loyola, "The Contemplation to Attain Love," Third point, *Spiritual Exercises* #236.

13. Ignatius of Loyola, "The Incarnation," First prelude, *Spiritual Exercises* #101.

very ordinary and the very demanding in human life. On the contrary, that is where God is to be found. God in the Incarnation and in his providence is progressively moving into and among these things. That is where God is. This is what God is doing. A human being, then, is to find God not in spite of all things, but in all things—to find God where God is actually present and acting and directing, that is, in all created things. One is united with God as God is—immanently working out the salvation of human beings.

Part Two: Human Response and Practice

And this brings us to the second of our coordinates: the human response to God so conceived and imaged. Let us look at this in its general sweep and then in the direction it gives to a life of prayer. Once again, let us do it schematically.

I. Does our "apprehension" of God make a difference in the way we are consciously united with God? Very much so, and perhaps the strongest way to realize this is in the metaphors in which these spiritualities propose union with God. Ascent spirituality often places its greatest focus on the bridal metaphor, the union of the bride with the spouse; incarnational or descent spirituality, on instrumental causality, the union of the human being with God in a single action that moves from God through the person into the world.[14] The person in this union is the one through whom God comes into a new influential presence, directing the world of matter and history.

A. In the first, the spouse draws the bride to himself until the passionate love he evokes has passed through purifying sufferings to reach what John of the Cross called "the spiritual marriage." In incarnational or descent spirituality, the soul

---

14. See Michael J. Buckley, S.J., "Ecclesial Mysticism in the Spiritual Exercises: Two Notes on Ignatius, the Church, and Life in the Spirit," *Theological Studies* (September/December 1995).

gives itself over to Christ and through Christ to God so that God can work in and through it, entering in this way into human history and all human enterprises. In both cases, there is union with God.

B. In both spiritualities, God is found—or rather, God finds the soul. And the person is united with God as God *de facto* is: either as the One evoking the soul to ascend to transcendent love or as the One who in love extends himself into human history and finite matter as their immanent—even governing—providence, becoming a part of this world finally through incarnation. In this latter, this incarnational spirituality, one follows the movement of God into the world.

C. This has enormous consequences in determining both the adoring consciousness of God that we call "prayer" and the consciousness of things that we call "detachment." Indeed, it profoundly affects the total way we live our lives and the projects and enterprises to which we dedicate our efforts under the perceived guidance of God.

D. Religiously, there is *one* work of grace going on. God is at work, giving himself. God is the single, principal agent to transform human beings in grace and human society in justice and peace. Those who give themselves over to this God in this work then become the means or the instruments through whom God works this effect. That is why Ignatius understood human religious causality as *instrumental*, just as Thomas Aquinas understood the *humanity* of Christ. "Instrumental" does not mean the autonomous or impersonal. The whole person is involved and the instrumentality is like that of the doctor in the restoration of health or of the teacher in the dispositions for gaining knowledge.

E. Of crucial importance to our apostolic mission is how deep this union between God and the human person, the means through whom God works, becomes.[15] The human is the personal instrument of the divine. It is one action that passes from God through those who serve him into the world that God loves. The mystical union is *in* this ministry, *in* this service. One becomes a contemplative also in activity, as Nadal insisted Ignatius had become.[16] This union allows God's presence and God's action to flow through human beings into the world.

II. The world then becomes the arena of this spirituality in a manner significantly like the event of the Incarnation. If incarnational spirituality understands God primarily and fundamentally within God's descent into matter, time, and place, into human choice, experience, and history through the Incarnation and through his immanent providence, then everything in human life becomes the concern of Christian spirituality.

A. The desire to allow God a deeper presence in human life, a more radical incarnation, is the conviction that lies behind the Church's interventions in such things as the structure and constituents of society, its advocacy of economic and political justice, its concern for international societies, education, art, and a more humane life. To be involved in these

---

15. Let me cite at some length from the last part of the *Constitutions*: "The Society was not instituted by human means; and neither is it through them that it can be preserved and developed, but through the omnipotent hand of Christ, God and our Lord....For the preservation and development not only of the body or exterior of the Society, but also of its spirit, and for the attainment of the objective it seeks, which is to aid souls to reach their ultimate and supernatural end, *the means that unite the human instrument with God and so dispose it that it may be wielded dexterously by His divine hand* are more effective than those which equip it in relation to men. Such means are, for example, goodness and virtue, and especially charity, and a pure intention of the divine service, and familiarity with God our Lord in spiritual exercises of devotion, and sincere zeal for souls for the sake of glory to Him who created and redeemed them and not for any other benefit" (*Constitutions* X. #812-813. [ET: Ganss]).

16. See Joseph F. Conwell, S.J. *Contemplative in Action. A Study in Ignatian Prayer* (Spokane, Washington: Gonzaga University), 1955.

areas is to foster the kingdom of God, and one component of that kingdom is a just social order. This has always to some degree been present in Christian convictions. One finds it in spiritualities that range from the ordinary social teaching of the Church to massive movements such as liberation theology. What incarnational spirituality insists upon is that God is here, that God is working here, that God would be more present through his union with you.

B. Perhaps the massive and comprehensive sweep that focuses incarnational spirituality received its most authoritative statement in the opening assertion of *Gaudium et Spes*:

> *The joy and the hope, the grief and the anguish of the human beings of our time, especially of those who are poor or afflicted in any way, are the joy and hope, the grief and anguish of the followers of Christ as well. Nothing that is genuinely human fails to find an echo in their hearts.*[17]

The concern is comprehensive:
> *It is for "the whole human family seen in the context of everything that envelops it. It is the world that is the theater of human history, bearing the marks of its travail, its triumphs and failures."*[18]

C. The Incarnation touches everything; providence governs everything. The dynamism of incarnational spirituality is to follow the directions of the Incarnation and the providence of God, indeed, to find God so deeply at work in all things: in the world of poverty and exploitation and social justice, in the world of art and education, in the world of inquiry, discovery and technical, scientific advance, in the world of

---

17. *Gaudium et Spes* (Pastoral Constitution on the Church in the Modern World), no 1.
18. Ibid., no. 2.

the family of human loves and friendship. God is at work in all things.

D. The essential questions: How can one find that presence and so collaborate with its influence and follow its direction? How can we find God there? How can we find God here? How can we grow in the experience and awareness of that presence and guidance?

Part Three: How Can We Find God in All Things?

That question would take vast acres of time to answer. Even the meaning of the phrase "to find God in all things" is itself not all that clear. I should like to suggest that it classically seems to speak to three interrelated moments in very ordinary Christian experiences of prayer.

I. First of all, the "finding of God" denotes a "way of meditating," a religious awareness that can be many things: [1] It can mean the contemplation or meditation occupying formal periods of prayer—which one could call the "spiritual exercises of devotion." This is what people usually mean when they talk about their prayer as this is brought to bear upon the thousands of things in their lives. [2] This religious awareness can refer to the discerning of the religious influences upon one's life, especially the influence of the Spirit of God calling us and directing us. This is what we normally speak about as the discernment of spirits which leads to a choice. [3] Religious awareness can refer to an atmospheric consciousness of a horizon and a presence in which the entire day is to be lived.[19] In this sense, religious awareness is a subtle sense as we go about our day that God is present, even though we might not advert to that presence explicitly very often. We know it is there. It is "nonthematic" prayer.

---

19. *Constitutions* X. #813.

A. Ignatius deals with the latter, for example, when he cut down the formal prayer of scholastics. Their normal exercises of piety should include daily Mass, an hour for formal prayer and examination of conscience, weekly confession, and Communion, and then:

> *They can exercise themselves in seeking the presence of our Lord in all things, as for example in conversing with someone, in walking, looking, tasting, hearing, understanding, and in all that they do, since it is true that His Divine Majesty is in all things by His presence, power, and essence. And this manner of meditating, by finding God our Lord in all things, is much easier than raising oneself to divine things that are more abstract and which require more effort to make them present to ourselves. Furthermore, this splendid practice will dispose us for greater visitations of our Lord, even in prayers that are rather short.*"[20]

B. Please note Ignatius does not mention any object for contemplation of a specifically religious nature. And he seems to take it for granted that this consciousness of God in concrete things is far easier than the kind of prayer that considers God apart from creation. But above all notice that there is no advice in Ignatius to forget the things and events around one at times of prayer and ascend to the darkness of God out of whom all things come. We have noted such an "ascent" is the theme of many profound and effective spiritualities and advice in prayer. It is not in the incarnational tradition and is exactly contrary to Ignatius's advice to the scholastics. They are to descend into the ordinary things of their

---

20. Ignatius to Anthony Brandao, MHSI.MI. *EppIgn* III, 506-513, Letter #1854. ET: William J. Young, S.J., *Letters of St. Ignatius of Loyola* (Chicago: Loyola University Press, 1959), 240.

lives and to find the immanent God as the source of their religious meaning.

C. Lastly, it is a profoundly different view of the world, of all that one encounters and understands, to see it fundamentally not as corrupt or seductive or contemptible, but as gift, and holy, and so sacramentally involved in sacred history that it forms the subject matter for our prayer.

II. Second, this religious awareness is conjoined to another kind of prayer—one that most of us grew up with—a kind of prayer that also involves "all things": the offering of one's day and work to God, the worship that is purity of intention, the activity that is purity of heart.

A. Here incarnational spirituality is taken up above all in the Mass, precisely as sacrifice. For Christ's offering of himself through the passion, death, and resurrection is a single, abiding offering. His offering is made present each time the Eucharist is celebrated as the Eucharist announces the death of the Lord until he comes. And his sacrifice is made present at this time and this place so that this community of Christians can offer their own lives to God in union with this single offering of Christ. This is to celebrate our covenant with God, to bind this part of our day and of our lives to the offering of Jesus with God. Much of this we learned as children in the remarkably profound content of the "Morning Offering," in which we offer our prayers, thoughts, words, actions, and sufferings to God—another set of ways in which we find God in all things.

B. In this self-offering one finds God, but finds in God the divine providence that encloses one's life and to which one is to give oneself.

III. Finally, there is the wordless prayer of affectivity. Here one finds God neither as the object of consciousness nor as the recipient of offering, but in a movement of sensibility. You will recall that Paul, in his Letter to the Galatians, gives a series of signs by which one can recognize the presence of the Spirit of God within one's experience. He called these signs the fruits of the Spirit and listed among them "love, joy, peace, patience, kindness, generosity, faithfulness, gentleness, and self-control" (Galatians 5:22-23a). These mark the spirit in which one lives and acts, which one chooses and communicates to others. They give an affective awareness of God's presence and evoke a response to that dynamic presence.

IV. What then, in summary, is meant by the phrase "to find God in all things"? One of at least three things; normally all three together: [1] a contemplative or discerning awareness of this immanent, working God, of the providence of God, the kind of prayer that moves from verbal to wordless contemplation; [2] an offering of oneself generously to be with God in this work, to offer oneself as one through whom may work as he wills; [3] an affective sense of responsive love and co-presence, what John of the Cross calls a "vague, general loving knowledge of God." All three are the human awareness of God at work in all things, of the providential, incarnate God who is found and in his descent into our history and our lives.

Conclusion

I cannot conclude without insisting that there is never a "pure" incarnational spirituality nor a pure ascent spirituality. These are rather critically important moments in any Christian spirituality, moments that will interact with one another to shape a spirituality appropriate for each person and community. Each of the spiritualities in the Church, I suspect, are a mixture of both of them—with emphasis given in various spiritualities to one rather than other. This was true, for example, of Ignatius, whom I have cited often in this lecture as an example of incarnational spirituality. Yet one should note the eremitic nature of the *Spiritual Exercises* and their withdrawal of the exercitant from all friends and relatives and from "all world care." And the reason for this total withdrawal: "The more the soul is in solitude and seclusion, the more fit it renders itself to approach and be united with its Creator and Lord; and the more closely it is united with Him, the more it disposes itself to receive graces and gifts from the infinite goodness of its God."[21] It must be the object of the discernment of spirits and of spiritual direction to discover the synthesis of spiritualities appropriate to an individual person's movement towards God.

---

21. Ignatius of Loyola, *The Spiritual Exercises,* "Annotation 20," [ET: Puhl].

4. Spirituality and the Human Creature

Sr. Mary Ann Hinsdale, I.H.M., Boston College

Introduction

The title of this essay might lead one to believe that I am going to talk about something that has just crawled out of "the black lagoon." At least, this is what was conjured up in my mind when Richard Miller sent me the title: "Spirituality and the Human Creature." I am probably dating myself here, but perhaps some of you are old enough to remember the same movies I watched as a teenager while babysitting on Saturday nights, called "Creature Features"? In any case, my reaction bears witness to one of the legacies of "modernity," namely, that most of us have a certain discomfort with the notion of human "creaturehood." Modifications of gender, race, class, and other particularities of our personal histories might modify the degree of our discomfort, but one look at the advertising that dominates today's media would corroborate this anxiety. I'm thinking particularly of those fantasy car ads for which there is no terrain too rough or remote for lightning-like speed and deft navigation: zoom, zoom, zoom!

Confronting the fact that we are not the independent, autonomous, "in-control" beings that our scientific, western, technological imagination has led us to think we are makes us uneasy. As human beings we resist encounters with our own finitude: Is that a gray hair I saw in the mirror this morning? Is that a hair *there*, where there never was one before? Where has all my hair gone? Should I really have let my seventeen-year-old drive the new car with his friends to the movies last night? And so on.

We struggle throughout our lives with such daily human questions, as well as the deeper ones: Who am I?, What do I long for?,

What am I doing with my life? All of these questions, from the truly sublime to the seemingly trivial, ultimately come down to questions of our own identity, meaning, and purpose. Those of us who have been alive for several decades or more know that, more frequently than we care to admit, we find ourselves a bit at sea, particularly in today's postmodern culture.

Our self-understanding tends to shift as we grow older. Perhaps we find that, after all, we are not really suited for the work we made the goal of our lives. Maybe we discover one day that the person we thought we knew—and loved—when we got married seems to have changed. Maybe I wake up one day and realize *I* have changed. Or, the Church to which I have devoted my entire life and whose shortcomings I may have even come to accept finally seems incapable of being the source of hope and inspiration that I need now. Such musings, if attended to, inevitably lead us to reflect on our lives and to search for a spiritual compass to guide our journey.

Religious traditions are particularly valuable in providing us with metaphors in our search for identity. My friend Jane Kopas, a Franciscan theologian who recently retired from the University of Scranton, reminds us in her book *Sacred Identity: Exploring the Theology of the Person*[1] that "creaturehood" is one of Christianity's key metaphors. We are creatures in relation to a divine creator. But what exactly does this mean? What does it mean to say I am *human*? That I am *created*? That I am *blessed* (graced) even though I am also a *sinner*?

The area of theology that explores the many facets of what it means to be human is traditionally called "theological anthropology," or sometimes simply "Christian anthropology." In standard textbooks of systematic theology, this division of theology is a foundational discipline. It is concerned with understanding the

---

1. Jane Kopas, *Sacred Identity: Exploring the Theology of the Person* (New York: Paulist Press, 1994).

meaning of human existence within the context of Christian revelation. Ever since the shift in Western philosophy known as "the turn to the subject," reflection upon human nature or personhood has become a natural corollary for theological reflection on the doctrines of God, creation, human embodiment, sin, the person and work of Jesus Christ (that is, Incarnation and redemption), grace, and eschatology.

Briefly, theological anthropology attempts to address a number of key questions about what it means to be human: What is God's intent and purpose for creation? What are the implications of the damage done to human potential due to the "the fall" of humanity? What is the process of restoration that God has made available to us in Christ? Four basic approaches/assumptions/principles ground most of the standard approaches to Christian anthropology:

1. An affirmation of the goodness of God and God's creation (especially the creation of humanity in God's image and likeness)
2. An affirmation that humanity has fallen short of the Creator's expectations (sin and the wrongly ordered operation of the human will which leads to the perpetuation of sin in the world, including human refusal to respect our interdependence with all created beings)
3. The observation of both the individual and communal aspects of goodness and evil, accounting for them in various ways, but ultimately concluding a) that goodness occurs through the operation of grace and b) that evil results through various aspects of the human condition, particularly through the exercise of human freedom
4. The attachment of understanding of human nature to the saving work of Jesus Christ, understood as a circular movement beginning with creation out of God's own self (what Karl Rahner would call "the self-communication of God"), the disobedience and fall of created beings, and the restoration to God in Christ

(which is to say that no understanding of human nature can be seen as operating independently of Christ)[2]

As a foundational theological discipline, theological anthropology provides us with the basic grounding for what we believe about worship, spirituality, ethics, and pastoral care.

But this is a conference on spirituality, not systematic theology! So that makes a difference in the language I would like to use. If one believes that spiritual life involves our encounter with God *within* our own human experience—and I do—then it is important to begin there and not with the many centuries of collective theological wisdom. Certainly I do not intend to ignore theological wisdom, since the whole purpose of this day is to see how our spirituality is rooted in the Church's tradition. However, I am reminded that Thomas Merton, for example, finally abandoned the attempt to talk about his experience of God and the contemplative life by using theological categories and instead, consciously turned to autobiography, literature, and poetry. Merton wrote:

> *I found in writing* The Ascent to Truth *that technical language does not convey what is most personal and most vital in religious experience. Since my focus is not upon dogmas as such, but only on their repercussions in the life of a soul in which they begin to find a concrete realization, I may be pardoned for using my own words to talk about my own soul.*[3]

This is something that I hope each of you will do for yourself, for your students, for your children and grandchildren, for your

---

2. For an in-depth consideration of these principles, see Gillian T. W. Alghren, ed., *The Human Person and the Church* (Maryknoll, N.Y.: Orbis Books, 1999).

3. Thomas Merton, *The Sign of Jonah* (New York: Harcourt Brace, 1953), 8-9. Cited by Sandra M. Schneiders, "A Hermeneutical Approach to the Study of Christian Spirituality," *Christian Spirituality Bulletin* 2 (1994): 11.

parishioners and your colleagues in ministry. By sharing your own spiritual story, you will contribute to the *sensus fidelium*, the sense of the faithful. The *sensus fidelium* is an important criterion for the communal discernment that the Church as People of God so desperately needs in our postmodern world. I encourage you to use your own words to talk about your spiritual life. Whatever fruits you gain from this day, I hope you will reflect upon the way God has interacted with you in the story of *your own life*. Who is the God that I experience? Where have I been drawn out of "dead ends" (self-absorption, fruitless obsessions, fears and anxiety) and saved from falling into a void of nothingness? Where have I experienced, in the revelation of my own vulnerability, a sense of compassion for others and the unexpected joy of being able to be a gift for someone else?

In looking for the answers to these questions in the concrete story of our own individual existences, as well as in our collective story as Church, I am convinced that we will be led, as were the authors of the Scriptures and the many saints who have left us the stories of their own spiritual journeys, to a better understanding of ourselves and the God who has called us into being and without whom we would cease to exist.

So many great spiritual teachers who have gone before us have left us the story of their souls: Thomas Merton, Dorothy Day, Thérèse of Lisieux, Teresa of Avila, Ignatius of Loyola, Julian of Norwich, Francis of Assisi, Benedict of Nursia, Teresa Benedicta of the Cross. Their life testimonies bear witness to another overlooked doctrine of the Catholic Tradition: the communion of saints. Vatican II reminded us that we are *all* called to holiness. All around us, whether they are officially canonized or not, there are living saints. Believing in the doctrines concerning human personhood—that we are created, prone to sin, yet transformed by God's grace—should embolden us to tell the story of the ways we have experienced these realities. So, I hope you will pardon me if I do not assume the role of systematic theologian here, but rather, share with you some fruits I have learned from wise teachers in the spiritual traditions which have influenced me personally.

I. Teachers of Spiritual Wisdom

A. Ignatian Spirituality from Karl Rahner

One of the first spiritual teachers I want to mention is Karl Rahner, the German Jesuit who, probably more than any other theologian, contributed so much to the renewal of Catholic theology in the twentieth century. Although most people tend to think of Rahner as a systematic theologian, what I most appreciate him for is his insight that God, who is absolute mystery, is nevertheless experienced in everyday life. Rahner developed a new and comprehensive way of viewing the various elements of Christian faith as one fundamental mystery: God's self-gift to the world. If we human creatures are made in the image and likeness of God (*imago Dei*), then we, too, are a mystery. Rahner's theological anthropology holds that the divine self-gift "is offered universally to all persons, in our self-transcending subjectivity."[4] What this means is that as human beings we come to know God in our knowledge and freedom. Our freedom, in Rahner's understanding, is not the ability to choose this or that, but the power to determine ourselves in a fundamental way, in our orientation to God. This work of "self-determination" becomes the work of our entire lives and, as a great Rahnerian scholar, Anne Carr, put it, "the score is never settled until the moment of death when what we have done with our lives, in response to God's self gift, becomes

---

4. Anne Carr, "Unsystematic Systematician," *Commonweal* (January 25, 1985): 43. I am indebted to this essay of Carr for what follows on Rahner. For further background in Rahner's theology, see Leo O'Donovan, ed., *A World of Grace: An Introduction to the Themes and Foundations of Karl Rahner's Theology* (New York: Crossroad, 1981). For a more recent introduction, see Declan Marmion and Mary E. Hines, eds., *The Cambridge Companion to Karl Rahner* (Cambridge: Cambridge University Press, 2005).

definitive. Freedom, experience, and history make our world, until its end, an open, unfinished work calling for our responsible creativity."[5] How it all enfolds, of course, belongs to the mystery we call life. And we learn throughout our lives, to cite Carr again, that "for all of our human planning, the future, God's future, cannot be controlled. Freedom and experience in history make all Christian theology open and unfinished. No system can comprehend life, especially the mystery of God's life in time."[6]

In some ways, Rahner was a most "unsystematic" theologian. He never wrote a multi-volume tome that tried to sum up in a grand narrative the meaning of everything. Rather, he wrote essays, called "theological investigations," in which he would deal with contemporary questions that arose from the experience of individual Christians and the Christian community as a whole. Rather than merely repeat the worn-out formulas of doctrine, as the Neo-scholastic, Christian apologetics of his time did—something which he felt was a distortion of the dynamic understanding of Tradition—Rahner tried to root theology in history, particularly in the spirituality, preaching, and tradition of Christian life. By focusing on the present Christian reality in light of the wisdom of the past, Rahner believed that contemporary Christians could discover the work of the Spirit in what we are experiencing *now* and carry that tradition forward.

I love to have students who are studying Rahner's anthropology read the following passage from his short essay, "Reflections on the Experience of Grace":

> *Have we ever actually experienced grace? We do not mean by this some pious feeling, a sort of festive religious uplift, or any soft comfort, but precisely the experiencing of grace, i.e., of that visitation by the Holy spirit of the triune God which has*

---

5. Carr, "Unsystematic Systematician," 43.

6. Ibid.

become a reality in Christ through his becoming man on the cross....Let us ask ourselves to begin with: have we ever experienced the spiritual?...We will perhaps answer: of course, I have experienced this....I think, I study, I make decisions, I act....In short, I know what spirit is. Yet it is not quite as simple as that....

Have we ever kept quiet, even though we wanted to defend ourselves when we had been unfairly treated? Have we ever forgiven someone even though we got no thanks for it and our silent forgiveness was taken for granted? Have we ever obeyed, not because we had to and because otherwise things would have become unpleasant for us, but simply on account of that mysterious, silent, incomprehensible being we call God and his will? Have we ever sacrificed something without receiving any thanks or recognition for it, and even without a feeling of inner satisfaction?...Have we ever tried to love God when we are no longer being borne on the crest of the wave of enthusiastic feeling, when it is no longer possible to mistake our self, and its vital urges, for God?...Have we ever been good to someone who did not show the slightest sign of gratitude or comprehension and when we also were not rewarded by the feeling of having been 'selfless,' decent, etc.?

...We have done so perhaps in a very anonymous and inexpressible manner.... But we know—when we let ourselves go in this experience of the spirit, when the tangible and assignable, the relishable element disappears, when everything takes on the taste of death and destruction, or when everything disappears as if in an inexpressible, as it were white, colorless and intangible beatitude—then in actual fact it is not merely the spirit but the Holy Spirit who is at work in us. Then is the hour of his grace.[7]

---

7. Karl Rahner, "Reflections on the Experience of Grace," *Theological Investigations*, vol. III (Baltimore: Helicon Press, 1967), 86-89.

These are just some of the places, Rahner tells us, where we can discover that it is not just the *human spirit* but the *Holy Spirit* who is at work in us. Such moments represent the hour of the Spirit's grace.

B. The Carmelite Tradition

Other teachers who have taught me about what it means to be human are the great saints of the Carmelite tradition. My order's spiritual heritage stems from that of Alphonsus Liguori, the founder of the Redemptorists. Alphonsus had a great devotion to Teresa of Avila, whom we IHM's (Sisters, Servants of the Immaculate Heart of Mary) take as one of our spiritual guides as well. The great saints of the Carmelite tradition—Teresa, John of the Cross, Thérèse of Lisieux, and Edith Stein—all put a high premium on "self-knowledge" as fundamental to spiritual growth. Thus, another important spiritual corollary of the doctrine of creation, of our "creaturehood," involves learning what my Carmelite friend Sr. Vilma Seelaus calls "the gentle vigilance of self-knowledge." Vilma recommends self-knowledge as an excellent form of asceticism—a word that may be out of vogue in our day, even if the practice certainly isn't. Just look at how much time we spend working out in gyms and on diets. Only now, those of us who remember being told before going out on a date that our bodies were "temples of the Holy Spirit" are working to keep them from turning into basilicas! Both John of the Cross and Teresa of Avila emphasize self-knowledge, though in different ways.

1. John of the Cross

For John, self-knowledge involves the realization that our very existence depends upon God's love. This can be an overwhelming realization, as Kees Waaijmen observes:

> *The road to God is not a road on which with much effort and exertion we meet the demands of God, but a journey on which we ever more deeply let ourselves be loved by God, in the*

realization that his love is unconditional. For that reason John of the Cross does not want to tell us all the things we have to do or not do in order to reach the love of God. Completely convinced of the love of God, he only wants to sing ecstatically of how God already loves us beforehand and totally. God's love does not depend on what we do: it is unconditional. God loves us in our very existence. After all, he is our existence and our life.[8]

In John of the Cross, the "dark night of the soul" involves a letting go of the old and embracing the "not yet" of the new; it is a dynamic process in between two stages. The night is a night of love—it is a night which makes the old world dark because something else, something more luminous, is being lit up in us which makes all other things relative. We experience this revelation as darkness because our human selves, unconditioned for the experience of God, are unable to take in the brightness of God. "The night symbolizes the bankruptcy of our grasping love, a love in which we ultimately only encounter ourselves. We take our leave from our own manner of loving so that God's love gets a chance to live in us."[9]

2. Teresa of Avila

Christian anthropology stresses a relational, embodied self, something that Teresa of Avila understood very well. But relatedness, Vilma Seelaus has written, "can be painful":

Although other persons reflect our uniqueness and help us discover our gifts and potential, they also mirror our inadequacies. As we struggle with the demands of friendship and

---

8. Hein Blommestijn, Jos Huls and Kees Waaijmen, *The Footprints of Love: John of the Cross as Guide in the Wilderness*, (Leuven: Peeters, 2000), 26.

9. Ibid.

human encounter, that relatedness undermines personal myths of omnipotence and reveals our finitude. The insecurity of finitude is hard to accept, and just as others willy-nilly make demands of us, we place all kinds of expectations on ourselves to be all-knowing and all-capable, to be fully adequate to every situation. Amid these usually unconscious self-expectations, the gifts and talents of others threaten us, so we turn them off or become defensive. Insofar as we are out of touch with these inner movements, envy, jealousy, and competitiveness keep us outside of the unifying energies of God's love that flow between people. The opposite can also happen. Self-doubt can so overwhelm us that we give up trying.[10]

But here is where the knowledge of our own imperfection actually can become the source of where God most wants to reveal the divine self in our lives. By looking squarely at "the emotional and attitudinal dams" that cause the loving flow of God in us to stagnate, we are strengthened by our self-knowledge

...to bear the pain of our failures as we struggle to learn new patterns of behavior more expressive of love. The asceticism of self-knowledge necessarily opens us to a deeper understanding of God in our life....God accepts us just as we are. Imperfection is normative to our finitude. For us to be perfect is to accept the reality of our imperfection.[11]

In her life, Teresa came to learn that the energy of God's creating love is more powerful even than sin and evil. We all struggle to make sense of evil, whether it be the violent destruction brought

---

10. Vilma Seelaus, "Asceticism and Chaste Celibate Love," *Review for Religious* 64 (2005): 171-72.

11. Ibid.,172.

about by human beings, such as the senseless murders experienced in the Oklahoma City bombing or 9/11, or the violence of nature in tornadoes, hurricanes, and tsunamis. Writing about her experience of the sixth dwelling place in *The Interior Castle*, Teresa tells how she was led to see all things *in God*:

> *Could the sinner, perhaps, so as to engage in his evil deeds leave this palace? No, certainly no; rather, within the place itself, that is, within God himself, the abominations, indecent actions, and evil deeds committed by us sinners take place....The greatest evil of the world is that God, our Creator, suffers so many evil things from his creatures within his very self and that we sometimes resent a word said in our absence and perhaps with no evil intention.*[12]

Today we, too, are called to recognize what these mystics have known: "that, in our universe and in the heart of every human person, there is an energy which as Christians we know to be God's creating love in all that exists."[13]

II. New Insights and Challenges: Christian Feminism and Ecological Theology

Thomas Berry, Sallie McFague, Elizabeth Johnson, Rosemary Ruether, and Ivone Gebara are just some of the theologians who have brought "the new cosmology" to our attention and who call us to examine how we human creatures think about ourselves in relation to the rest of God's creation. Feminist theologians, in particular, have reminded us of the ancient insight of the mystics, that we

---

12. Teresa of Avila, *Interior Castle*, VI. 10.2-3, in *Collected Works of St. Teresa of Avila*, vol. 2, trans. Otilio Rodriguez and Kieran Kavanaugh (Washington, D.C.: ICS Publications, 1980), 419.

13. Seelaus, "Asceticism and Chaste Celibate Love," 169.

will never be able to capture in words the mystery that is God. Let me offer two brief comments concerning the insights that Christian feminist theologies offer contemporary spirituality.

A. Christian Feminism

Christian feminist theologians writing today have pointed to the critical importance of retaining the ultimate unknowability of God. The persistent, almost exclusive, association of God with maleness in our traditional approaches to theology and worship has left the impression that we are able to know something quite definite about God in terms of gender. Thus, Jane Kopas warns:

> *Insistence on the maleness of God can lead to a new form of idolatry. Gender idolatry says that the only God worthy of worship is a male God. Those who make this assertion compensate for the hiddenness and incomprehensibility of God with an image that replaces the ultimacy of God. To let God be God, whatever we say of God, needs to be relativized in light of the hidden and incomprehensible creative source.[14]*

Surely, this insight challenges us individually and as a Church to rethink how we refer to God in our prayer and worship. The Scriptures, particularly the example of Jesus, as well as the writings of women mystics, give us many options for naming God.[15]

B. Ecofeminist Theology

According to Brazilan theologian Ivone Gebara, the central assumption of an ecological understanding of what it means to be human

---

14. Kopas, *Sacred Identity*, 74-75.

15. See, for example, Elizabeth Johnson, "Naming God She: The Theological Implications," *Princeton Seminary Bulletin* 22 (2001): 134-49; Mary Collins, "Naming God in Public Prayer," *Worship* 59 (1985): 291-304.

creatures is the interdependence that exists among all elements. This is an affirmation that comes from our own experience. We only need to attend to what takes place within our own bodies. When I am in pain, even the most habitual act becomes difficult. Anyone who has ever broken a rib knows how difficult it is to do something as normal and habitual as breathing. And if we have trouble breathing, how can we even think or express the love and tenderness we should have for our fellow creatures—human or non-human?

For Gebara, an ecofeminist perspective enables us to go beyond concern for our own bodies and become open to the greater body, which is God's body:

> *Interdependence means accepting the basic fact that any life situation, behavior, or even belief is always the fruit of all the interactions that make up our lives, our histories, and our wider earthly and cosmic realities. Our interdependence and relatedness do not stop with other human beings: They encompass nature, the powers of the earth and of the cosmos itself. In this sense, knowing is a human act insofar as it refers to the particular types of conscious processes and awarenesses that characterize the human being as a form of living organization. However, the animal, vegetable, and cosmic forms of consciousness are also part of our makeup. This other kind of interdependence does not come to full, conscious awareness, and so it is rarely considered. We do not recognize its importance because it seems obvious that we live in a given place and that in that place we breathe, eat, walk, and sit. Furthermore, our senses are seldom educated to perceive this interdependence's great importance. Once we do recognize its importance, however, we will be able to care for the earth and all its inhabitants as if they were close relatives, as parts of our greater body, without which individual life and consciousness are impossible.[16]*

Conclusion

In this brief presentation, I have tried to:

1. Outline the various doctrines that make up the theological discipline called "Christian anthropology"
2. Draw upon some of my own personal, "favorite spiritual traditions": Ignatian spirituality (as expressed through Karl Rahner) and the Carmelite mystics Teresa of Avila and John of the Cross (with the help of Vilma Seelaus)
3. Merely allude to two movements, signs of our own times: the emergence of women rightly claiming their participation in *imago Dei* and the need to bring a new lens to how we, as creatures, are interdependent with all created reality. The clarifications, modifications and refinements to the doctrinal themes of Christian anthropology that these two cultural and intellectual movements ("signs of the times") present are still being worked out in theology today

Since we are the human beings—the human creatures—living in an age so affected by these developments, it is incumbent upon us to share the story of how God has called us into being: as women, as men, as earth-dwellers in an ever-expanding universe.

---

16. Ivone Gebara, *Longing for Running Water: Ecofeminism and Liberation* (Minneapolis: Fortress Press, 1999), 52.

5. Spirituality and Redemption

Rev. Michael J. Himes, Boston College

Few themes are more identified with Christian spirituality than redemption. To begin consideration of the theme, we must sort out some vocabulary. Often we run certain terms together as though they all mean the same thing, when in fact they carry quite different connotations. Three words which we need especially to clarify are redemption, salvation, and atonement. Frequently we speak of Jesus as being the source of our redemption, of Jesus as our Savior, and of Jesus making our atonement with God, as if all three are effectively synonymous. While the three notions are certainly related, they are not simply identical. In fact, they carry somewhat different connotations.

Redemption is largely a legal theme. It refers to the idea of redeeming a pledge. For example, I request a loan from someone and leave my property as a pledge of my good faith in repaying the loan. When I pawn something I own, I am expected to redeem my pledge. I must buy it back, as it were, by repaying the debt I have incurred. Redemption is a metaphor, an image, which we use to imply that Jesus has paid our debt and so ransomed us back to God. The metaphor is a legal procedure.

The theme of salvation, however, is closely associated with a term that may be more familiar to Catholics at the end of the twentieth and the beginning of the twenty-first century: liberation. Salvation suggests freeing someone from a burden. It derives from the Latin *salus*, which primarily means "health" or "well-being." It is rooted in the image of freeing people from some burden that encumbers or oppresses them, such as an illness or a disease, a pain or a problem. It has to do with making people free and whole again. By contrast to the legal metaphor of redemption, salvation is originally a medical image.

Atonement is a medieval English word meaning, literally, "at-one-ment." It has to do with bringing people into reconciled communion with one another, leading those who were for some reason separated from one another and making them at-one with one another. The metaphor is that of the establishment of peaceful union. As redemption is a legal metaphor for what God has done for us in Christ, and salvation a medical metaphor, atonement is a social, political (in the root sense of organizing a community), even familial metaphor. Thus we have three quite different images for thinking and speaking about what Jesus has done for us: buying us back; healing us, liberating us, freeing us from an oppressive burden; and bringing us into communion with God and one another, establishing peaceful union.

These three metaphorical ways of speaking about what God has done for us in Christ complement one another. Their interaction has produced different ways of considering Jesus' redeeming or saving or atoning work. I shall briefly mention three such ways of considering Jesus' work that have been put forth in the Church's history and note their strengths and problems. I shall then suggest a fourth and mention why I think it may be both more congruous with the biblical witness to what is accomplished in Jesus' life, death, and resurrection and also more faithful to the Catholic Tradition. To illustrate this, I shall ask you to consider a familiar New Testament parable in light of this fourth way of understanding what salvation or redemption or atonement mean.

In 1930, Gustaf Aulén, a distinguished Lutheran scholar, published a book that has become something of a modern classic in theology: *Christus Victor*.[1] The title suggests a traditional biblical image: Christ the victor over sin and death. Throughout his scholarly career, Aulén was concerned to trace out the essential motifs underlying Christian doctrinal formulas. In *Christus Victor*, he took

---

1. Gustaf Aulén, *Christus Victor* (London, 1930; New York; Macmillan Co. 1951).

up the question of what it means to say that we are saved by Jesus. What are we saved from, and how is this salvation accomplished? He outlined three theories of the salvific work of Jesus that have been prominent in the Church's history. Because Aulén's description of these various theories of salvation has become so standard in theology, I shall follow them here.[2] Aulén referred to the classical theory, the Latin or (as others have named it) the transactional theory, and the subjective theory.[3]

The Classical Theory

The classical theory is found in the writings of the Fathers of the Church. To be sure, there are as many variations as there are patristic writers on the topic of the salvation worked in Christ. Nevertheless, certain elements are common to almost all the Fathers. From what are we saved? The usual patristic response is from the power of the devil. Through sin—our personal sins or that of the first human beings—we have chosen to give our allegiance to Satan rather than to God. Instead of listening to God's word and obeying God's will, Adam and Eve chose—and in countless ways we have chosen—to trust Satan rather than God. The story of the Fall in Genesis 3 recounts the serpent's telling the first human beings that, despite God's warning that eating of the tree of the knowledge of good and evil will bring death, eating the tree's fruit will in fact make them like God. The choice is clear: Are human beings to trust God or the serpent? And the first human beings choose to believe the serpent. They—and we—have given allegiance and placed trust in Satan

---

2. Many other writers have followed Aulén's classification even while refining or adding to it. Noteworthy are Edward Yarnold, *The Second Gift* (Slough: Saint Paul Publications, 1974) and Michael Winter, *The Atonement* (Collegeville: Liturgical Press, A Michael Glazier Book, 1995).

3. Yarnold offers a fourfold classification: Atonement as Conflict, Atonement as Transaction, Atonement as Enlightenment, and Atonement as Solidarity (*The Second Gift*, 109ff.). Winter discusses these and offers a fifth: Atonement as Intercession (*The Atonement*, 87ff.).

rather than God. We have become Satan's followers, as it were, and so we are part of Satan's dominion. We must be rescued from Satan, bought out of slavery to Satan, redeemed from our voluntary bondage. That is Jesus' work. He redeems us from the power of evil. How does Jesus redeem us? Various patristic authors give slightly different answers.

Perhaps the most colorful account is that offered by Gregory of Nyssa (approximately 330-395), one of the Cappadocian Fathers, great teachers of the fourth century. In several of his sermons, Gregory gives a very dramatic, highly mythological account of how Jesus redeems us.[4] Because we abandoned our rightful fidelity to God and gave allegiance to Satan, God withdrew life from us, and so we became subject to death. The wages of sin is death, and because we are all sinners, Satan has the right to put us to death. Because the Son has assumed human nature, Jesus appears to be a human being and a sinner just like the rest of us, although, in reality, he is like us in all things except sin. Because Satan assumes that Jesus has inherited the guilt of Adam and is a sinner like all other human beings, Satan mistakes him for one who is justly subject to the penalty of death. And so Satan seizes him and has him put to death, and in doing so is tricked into overstepping his rights over sinful humanity since, of course, Jesus is the one human being who does not deserve death. By having exceeded his rights over humanity, Satan is deprived of his lordship over us. He has been found cheating, as it were, so the game is canceled and all the chips are returned to God's side of the table. Thus, we are redeemed by Jesus' death because, in killing Jesus, Satan oversteps his proper sway, and so we are redeemed from his power and restored to God's reign.

This is a dramatic story that has the advantage of impressing its hearers and being readily remembered by them. One of its principal strengths is that it echoes and develops a number of biblical images.

---

4. Gregory of Nyssa, *Catechetical Orations*, 21-24, *passim.*

As is so often the case with patristic preaching, there is strong scriptural resonance. There are, nevertheless, several problems with it as a theological account of our salvation in Christ. One striking oddity is the notion of Satan's having "rights" over creation that God must in some way respect. The obvious danger with such thinking is that it can seem to make Satan a rival power to God. This is, of course, nonsense: God is *God*. God has no rival. Second, the imagery of God resorting to a kind of trickery in order to overcome Satan's dominion over creation is simply bizarre. It reduces God to a sharp operator who allows Satan to be deceived for a good purpose. Indeed, the great biblical exegete and theologian Origen (approximately 185-254), who exerted a strong influence on many later patristic writers including Gregory of Nyssa, employed the striking image of the redemption as being like landing a fish. God disguised the hook of the Son's divinity by embedding it in the bait of our humanity and then dangled it before Satan who, like a hungry fish, lunged for it because he could see only another guilty human being deserving of death. Having swallowed Jesus' humanity, he was caught by Jesus' divinity. The divine hook landed the satanic fish.[5] These are wonderfully clever images that served as popular catechetical tools. They grasped people's attention and caught their imagination, but they have serious problems as a theological account of what it means to say that we are saved by Christ.

The Latin (or Transactional) Theory

One who perceived those serious problems was Anselm of Canterbury (1033-1109), a very important figure in the history of the Church's reflection on salvation. A teacher and later abbot at the Benedictine abbey of Bec in Normandy and subsequently Archbishop of Canterbury, Anselm was deeply dissatisfied with these patristic

---

5. Origen, *Commentary on Matthew's Gospel*, 13, 8-9. Gregory of Nyssa also employed the bait-and-hook analogy. See his *Catechetical Orations*, 21-24.

approaches to atonement theory for the reasons I have mentioned. He thought that a new understanding was needed, one that avoided any notion of God's negotiating with the devil, or Satan's having rights over creation, or God's resorting to trickery to destroy Satan's dominion. His attempt at a better theology of redemption is *Cur Deus homo* (*Why God Became Man*), a great classic in the history of theology. His answer to the implied question in his title was that only one who is fully divine and fully human could accomplish our redemption. Anselm's theory was destined to have a long life and a wide influence in the Western Church. I suspect that it is familiar to many if not most western Christians, both Catholic and Protestant, who have never read or perhaps heard of Anselm.

In Anselm's view, we are creatures of God, that is, God has made us out of nothing. We are utterly, totally, completely dependent on God. What therefore do we owe God? Quite literally, everything. So, if we rebel against God, if we disobey God, our fault is infinite because our debt to God is infinite. If we turn away from God, our sin is of infinite gravity both because God whom we offend is infinite and what we owe God is infinite. Thus our guilt is limitless and the penalty we must pay is infinite. If our sin is an infinite fault because we sinned against an infinite Good to whom we owe an infinite debt, how are we finite creatures to make it up? We should remember that Anselm was writing at the end of the eleventh century in the world of medieval feudalism. In that very hierarchical world, the gravity of the injury done is in proportion to the dignity of the one injured. Thus, for a serf to offend another serf is bad, but for a serf to offend his lord is worse. In such a worldview, the gravity of a creature offending against the Creator is immeasurable. How can such a depth of guilt be made up? Since human beings have committed the offense, clearly a human being must make good the damage. Since the damage is infinite, however, we human beings cannot possibly pay the debt. For if we were to give all that we are to God, we would only be giving what we creatures owe our Creator in the first place. We have nothing with which we can make good the debt our sin has incurred. Only one who is of infinite worth could repair our guilt by offering himself as a gift to God, that is, only God can make infinite recompense for infinite guilt. Since the damage was done by human beings, however, only a human being ought to make the recompense. The payment of our debt to God—our redemption—and the removal of our guilt—our salvation—require one who is both fully and truly divine, and so of infinite worth, and fully and truly human, and so appropriate as the one who satisfies the debt. This is, in answer to the question in the title of Anselm's book, why the God-man. The Son becomes incarnate precisely in order to give his life in utter obedience and fidelity to the Father; as divine he can heal an infinite breach, and as human he should do so.[6]

Undeniably, there is great elegance in Anselm's theory of redemption. It is noteworthy that Satan has effectively disappeared from the story entirely. There is nothing whatever about paying a penalty to Satan or about God entering into negotiation with the devil. Nor does God have to outwit an enemy or delude an opponent with a clever trick. So Anselm avoids the most glaring difficulties of the classical patristic theory.

Anselm's theory has its own problems, however. While it is true that Anselm avoids any talk of a negotiation between God and the devil, he does so by transferring the image of paying satisfaction within the Trinity. Instead of God paying satisfaction to the devil on behalf of humanity, the Son renders satisfaction to the Father. Also, note that Anselm's account can lead—and in much of western spirituality has led—to the idea that the reason for the Incarnation, the reason Jesus is born, is precisely in order to die. Indeed, as Anselm presents his account of salvation accomplished in Christ, it appears that the only really significant events are Jesus' birth and death. In

---

6. See Anselm of Canterbury, *The Major Works*, ed. Brian Davies and G. R. Evans (Oxford: Oxford University Press, 1998), 260-356, esp. 282-320.

Cur Deus homo, no reference is made to Jesus' teaching, his preaching of the Kingdom, his miracles, his calling disciples, or his forming a community. All these are presumably ways by which we are edified and educated, but what saves us is that the Son unites to himself a human nature so that he can die and then that he actually does die. Surely this exclusive emphasis on Jesus' death rather than on his life and his preaching seems exaggerated. A third important point to notice about this theory of redemption is that it seems that our salvation is the result of a change in God rather than in us. The Son takes on our humanity and becomes incarnate, dies in obedience to the Father's will, and as a result the Father is reconciled with us. We human beings do nothing. Although this was certainly not Anselm's intention, his theory of the atonement requires a story of how God's attitude toward us changes, how God ceases to be alienated from us, rather than a story of how we are changed and are no longer alienated from God.

Despite these anomalies, Anselm's theory is probably the account of redemption that most western Christians, Catholic and Protestant, have been taught. It has shaped popular piety in the Western Church more than any other theory of the atonement. One of the best ways to discern the spirituality that shapes people's lives is to examine the hymns they sing. Long after people forget the catechism lessons they were taught and the homilies they heard, they remember the hymns they sang. And if one were to study much of our hymnody one will find its soteriology, its theology of atonement, is pure Anselm of Canterbury. Unfortunately, entirely against Anselm's intention, one cannot fail to notice how his theory of our salvation in Christ lends itself—when taken up by preachers and teachers far less theologically sophisticated, knowledgeable, and careful than Anselm himself—to the notion of an angry and vengeful God alienated from creatures because of their sinful disobedience who demands punishment. To appease the Father's anger, the Son becomes incarnate, suffers and dies in humanity's stead. God's law has been transgressed, and God's justice demands that someone suffer, if not sinners then the innocent incarnate Son. Indeed, in its worst form—and once again, we must recognize that this is a terrible distortion of Anselm's ideas—the depth of the Father's anger, the viciousness of human sin, and the greatness of Jesus' mercy are displayed not only by the fact of Jesus' death, but by the extremity of his suffering and final agony. This extreme emphasis on Jesus' suffering to appease the Father's anger promotes a truly ghastly image of God as a petulant parent determined that someone will be punished in order to assuage his outrage at being disobeyed. The Son volunteers to be punished in our stead, and after the Son has been sufficiently brutalized, the Father is appeased and extends forgiveness to creatures once again. This is much more Mel Gibson than Anselm of Canterbury, but sadly it is certainly part of many people's piety.

The Subjective Theory

The third theory that Aulén distinguished is the one he named the subjective; others have called it the theory of salvation as enlightenment. It is most often connected with Peter Abelard. Abelard, a distinguished scholar and famous teacher of theology in the first half of the twelfth century, seems to have taught (I say "seems" because it is not entirely clear what Abelard actually taught and what his critics understood him to have taught.) that in the Incarnation the Son has become human like us in order to show us how to live a truly faithful, loving, obedient human life. We see his obedience, even to death on a cross. The confusion and alienation caused by sin are pierced by this illuminating ray of Jesus' teaching and even more his example, and we must now follow that teaching and example and so come to salvation.[7]

There is much to be said for Abelard's theory but, as just

---

7. Abelard, *Commentary on the Epistle to the Romans*, 2 (Migne, *Patrologia Latina* 178: 1836). See the brief but perceptive discussion of Abelard in Winter, *The Atonement*, 68ff.

summarized, there is also a great problem. Abelard's contemporary, the great Cistercian abbot and theologian, Bernard of Clairvaux, saw the difficulty and scathingly attacked Abelard for it. If Abelard was simply maintaining that Jesus supplies us with his teaching and example and we then model ourselves on him, then when all is said and done, we save ourselves. Salvation consists in our work of following Christ's example. Jesus gives us the directions and we carry them out. The actual work of salvation is not done by Jesus but by us. If that was Abelard's position, Bernard was right. It certainly is not in accord with the Christian Tradition.

A Fourth Way: Jesus as Sacrament

The question is whether that really was Abelard's position, or, perhaps better, whether it was his intention. It may be that Abelard perceived something which he was unable to express in adequate categories. To explain this, it will be helpful to turn back to Anselm's position since clearly Abelard intended his position as a counter to it. It is something of a theological commonplace today to criticize the theory of atonement set out by Anselm of Canterbury. Throughout *Cur Deus homo*, he speaks very much in terms of redemption. As has been noted, redemption is a legal image: I must redeem something I have pawned with you as a pledge by paying what I owe you. Let us consider, however, points in Scripture when Jesus forgives someone, for example his encounters with the woman who washes his feet with her tears (Luke 7:36-50), with the Samaritan woman at the well (John 4:5-42), with Zacchaeus (Luke 19:1-10), or with the woman caught in adultery (John 8:1-11). There does not seem to be any suggestion of a debt that the sinner must make good before he or she is forgiven. Jesus never requires a sacrifice that must be offered before the sinner is reconciled with God. All that is required is that the sinner by word or by gesture requests forgiveness, and forgiveness is immediately granted. Anselm's image of redemption may make perfect sense in the social and political relationships of medieval feudalism, but it does not seem to resonate with the way Jesus forgives sin in the Gospel.

How may we understand our salvation in Christ, that is, the gift of forgiveness brought to us by Jesus, in a way that is faithful to the scriptural witness and deeply rooted in the Catholic tradition? I suggest two principles that must always be observed. The first principle is that, in whatever way we speak about the atonement (our being brought into peaceful communion with God), about our salvation (our liberation from the bondage of sin), we must tell the story as an account of how we are changed, not how God changes. If we tell a story of God who was distant from us and then drew closer, or who was offended and then assuaged, or who was angry and then relented, we are engaged in mythology, not Christian theology. The "God" about whom we would be speaking would be Zeus, not the Father of our Lord Jesus Christ. God is God. God does not change. You and I change, but God is God. So the first principle for understanding how we are saved is that we have been changed, not God.

The second principle brings me to a category that I suspect Abelard may have been groping toward but that was not developed in his day to the point that he could use it. I suggested that Abelard may have been feeling his way toward an important insight that he did not know how to express. I think that he was seeking for the classically Catholic category of "sacrament."

Central to the Catholic vision of the Christian tradition is the sacramental principle: that which is always and everywhere true must be noticed, accepted and celebrated somewhere sometime. What is always and everywhere true must be noticed, attended to, recognized as the case. It must be accepted, agreed to, embraced. And it must be celebrated, gratefully received concretely at some time and some place. For example, although we may love and value someone all the time, there are and must be particular occasions when we recognize and celebrate that fact, occasions like birthdays and anniversaries. If we love someone all the time, sometime we had better tell him or her. We speak of holy days and sacred seasons. There is, of course, nothing more intrinsically holy about Sunday than about any other day of the week. Since all time is God's time, however, sometime we must attend to the fact. We consecrate a building as a sacred place, for example a church or chapel, not because God is present there as opposed to anywhere else. God is everywhere. And precisely because God is everywhere, somewhere we must notice the fact. What is always and everywhere true must be noticed, accepted, and celebrated somewhere sometime. The necessity arises from the fact that usually what is universally acknowledged to be true is ignored. What "everyone knows" is taken for granted and so overlooked. What is always present is often ignored. We do not pay attention to the oxygen in a room until the air becomes stale. We do not notice our heart beating unless it skips a beat. What is always there is frequently unnoticed. We need persons, things, places, times, events, occasions that cause us to notice, to attend, to accept, to celebrate, and to give thanks for what is always present, and what is always present is grace.

"Grace" is the name traditionally given to the self-giving of God outside the Trinity. God's self-communication, the free gift of God's self, is the very reason that the universe exists. The only reason that anything other than God exists at all is that God loves it. God's perfect gift of self is the reason there is something rather than nothing. Everything that exists does exist because it is held in being by God's love; it is at every instant the recipient of God's self-communication. If something is not loved by God, it is not damned; it simply *is* not. Thus, at the root of all being, at the foundation of the universe, is God's self-gift, that is, grace. This is always and everywhere true. But what is always and everywhere true may go unnoticed unless something calls our attention to it somewhere sometime. We must attend to the reality of grace, accept it and gratefully celebrate it. The persons, places, things, events, sights, sounds, tastes, touches, and smells that cause us to attend to grace and invite us to accept and celebrate it are called sacraments. Certainly in the Catholic Tradition there are the seven great communal sacraments, but there are also the countless, personal sacraments which mark our lives. That this is so is entirely in accord with the sacramental principle.

It is this understanding of sacrament toward which I suggest Abelard was moving, although it did not receive its rich elaboration until the century after his time. We cannot think of the salvation accomplished in Jesus' life, death, and resurrection as a point before which God did not give God's self to us and after which God does. This is to run afoul of the first principle I have mentioned: however we consider salvation, we must not make it an account of how God is changed but rather how we are. God always gives God's self to us and to all creation. God has always loved us absolutely. If God did not, we and the rest of creation simply would not be. There was not a time when God did not forgive the human race and then a time when God did, although there may well have been a time when we did not accept being forgiven. God's forgiveness is omnipresent; it is always and everywhere. For that reason, sometime somewhere we must attend to being saved and forgiven, accept the freely given gift, and celebrate it. We must attend to, accept, and celebrate being loved and cherished and held in being by the endless gift of God's self. We must attend to, accept, and celebrate being "engraced." The ultimate expression of God's loving self-communication (gift of grace), and so of our salvation, is the life, death, and resurrection of Jesus Christ. His life, death, and destiny is the sacrament of our redemption. This is not to suggest, as Bernard of Clairvaux understood Abelard to have taught, that in Christ's obedience to the Father even to death on a cross we are given a good example that we then follow. Rather, it is to say that in Jesus' living and dying in accord with the Father's will we are given the full and perfect embodiment of the always-present, always-reconciling, gracious love of God poured out to all creatures. Because it is now incarnated in space and time, lived out perfectly in history, unsurpassably manifested before us, what had gone unrecognized is now presented to us in a way that we cannot ignore so that we may accept it with gratitude and celebrate it with joy. *If* that was what Abelard glimpsed and struggled to express, however inadequately, he was quite right.

This is the undoing of sin. Recall the biblical depiction of the origin of sin in Genesis 3. The first temptation in Genesis 3:4-5 is an invitation to disbelieve what we have heard two chapters earlier. In Genesis 1:26, the first thing said about human beings is that God has made us in God's image and likeness as the culmination of the universe which is repeatedly proclaimed "good" throughout the creation story. And the first temptation is not to believe that. The serpent insinuates to the first human beings that God has not made them "like God," as chapter one maintains. God-likeness, according to the serpent, must be earned, achieved, wrested from God. It is not a gift freely given but an accomplishment of our own. We are not created good; we must make ourselves good: "Eat this and you will be like God" (see Genesis 3:5). The primal temptation, the beginning of evil, is to refuse to believe that one is the object of God's love, the recipient of God's perfect self-gift. It is to think that we may be able to make ourselves good, to earn God-likeness, but that we certainly do not receive it purely and simply as a gift. Conversely, to say finally that we do not deserve it, we cannot earn it, we cannot achieve it and to believe that we are given God simply because God is God, pure and perfect self-gift—that is the moment of salvation. And that is sacramentalized in the life, death, and destiny of Jesus Christ.

To illustrate that this way of thinking about how we are saved by Christ is in accord with the New Testament description of the manner of Jesus' forgiveness of sinners, I turn to one of the most familiar parables of Jesus, the story of the Prodigal Son (Luke 15:11-32). Certainly it is a story that we all know. Please note, however, that the father remains unchanged in the course of the parable. Indeed, it is not entirely clear that that younger son changes very much either, but unquestionably the father does not.

Remember that in the highly patriarchal world of the ancient Near East one's whole status as a person—socially, familiarly, religiously, economically—depended on one's relationship to the head of the household: the father. Thus, the father was a sacred figure in the biblical world. With that in mind, the opening of the parable is shocking. A man had two sons, the younger of whom decided that he did not wish to remain tied to his home until his father finally died and who, therefore, asked that the estate be broken up during his father's lifetime so that he could enjoy his inheritance. Even today, in our far less patriarchal world, we might well find such a request outrageous. In the world of the New Testament, it was almost unthinkable. The response of any respectable parent would be to cut the younger son off without a nickel. But instead, we read that the father did precisely what the younger son requested: he divided the estate in two, turned half of it into cash and gave it to the son. The son went off to a foreign land and spent it on wine, women, and song. Then when a famine struck that land, he had nothing to live on and was forced to take a job tending pigs. No one gave him anything to eat, and he was so hungry that he coveted the slop being thrown to the pigs. It is useful to recall that this is a Jewish story told by a Jew to Jews. It is no mere detail that the younger son tended pigs, unclean animals according to the Mosaic code. In a Jewish story, to covet the food thrown to non-kosher animals is to have sunk as low as it is possible to go. It is a graphic image of having hit the bottom of the barrel. The younger son realized that at his home there was plenty of food and the servants ate well. And so he said to himself, "I know what I shall do. I will go to my father and say, 'Father, I have sinned against heaven and against you and am not worthy to be called your son. Treat me as one of your hired servants'" (see Luke 15:17-19). And so he set off. To understand fully the radical character of the parable, we must notice that the only motive given for his return home is that he can eat better there. There is not the slightest indication that he is sorry for his treatment of his father or that he misses his family. In fact, the selfishness of his motivation is underscored in the parable by the fact that he prepares his little speech to the father beforehand. So far as we can tell, the younger son is as self-centered at the end of the story as he was at its beginning.

The father saw the younger son approaching from a long way off. We—and I strongly suspect the first hearers and readers of the parable—might well think that a responsible parent would first ask where the younger son has been, why he looks so bedraggled, and where all the money he had been given is. But no, the father runs down the road to greet the son, who launches syllable for syllable into the prepared text: "Father, I have sinned against heaven and against you and am not worthy...." It is a wonderful touch in the parable that he never gets to the final line: "Treat me as one of your hired servants." The father cuts him off before that by ordering the servants to get the son a robe and sandals, to put a ring on his finger (a symbol of welcome and restored family status), and to kill the fatted calf for a celebratory dinner. The younger son is swept into the house for the party, and we hear no more of him in the story.

And now the third principal character in the parable makes his first appearance. The elder son returns from laboring all day on the family farm and hears the celebration going on in the house. When he asks one of the servants the cause, the servant replies in what I can only interpret as a tone dripping with sarcasm: "Your brother has come back after wasting a fortune, and your father is throwing a party." Presumably even the servants find the father's behavior bizarre. The elder son now does something shocking: He refuses to go in and eat with his father. For a son to refuse to sit down at table and break bread with his father, no matter who else was at the table, was unthinkable behavior in the ancient Near East. The father's response to this is what the hearer or reader has come to expect at this point in the story: He comes out to his elder son and, instead of ordering him or throwing him out, begins to plead with him. And now we arrive at the point toward which the whole parable has been moving. The older son complains that he has worked for his father faithfully and done whatever his father has asked of him, and the father has never given him so much as a kid goat to celebrate with his friends. Now his wastrel younger brother has returned having gone through half the family fortune and the fatted calf is slain to greet him. This is, of course, the ancient cry of all siblings: "It's not fair!" In reply, the father does not deny anything that his older son has said. He agrees that the older boy has always been faithful to him. But, he maintains, the one who was lost has been found. The one who was dead is alive. How could we not rejoice?

This conversation between the father and the elder son is the climax of the parable. Notice: this is not a parable about repentance or conversion because, as far as we told by the story, no one repents, no one converts. Rather, it is a parable about the incomprehensible goodness of God. This is why the father and the elder son seem to talk past one another. The son bases his complaint on justice, on being fair. The father never denies the importance of justice, but his position is rooted in agape, perfect self-gift. Recall the context of the parable in Luke's Gospel. The Pharisees have complained that Jesus associates at table with sinners, and in response Jesus tells them the parable (Luke 15:1-3).[8] That is why the parable culminates in a dispute about whom one will eat with at table. In effect, what Jesus is saying to the Pharisees is that, if they insist on thinking about God's relationship to sinful humanity as primarily that of law-giver, judge, dispenser of justice, then they will never understand who his Father is, because the primary metaphor for God is not justice but "agapic" love.

If we are to understand the atonement worked by Christ and incorporate it into our spiritual lives, we must not think of God as the One whose justice must be satisfied or whose wrath must be

---

8. In fact, Jesus replies to the Pharisees' charge with three parables: the Lost Sheep (Luke 15:4-7), the Lost Coin (Luke 15:8-10), and finally the Prodigal Son (Luke 15:11-32).

appeased. Indeed, we are probably more misled than helped by using legal or commercial categories like redemption. We must begin with the incomprehensible fact that God has always loved us and has always given God's self to us. That incomprehensible mystery of divine goodness and love and forgiveness is revealed, embodied, incarnated, and—using my term—sacramentalized in the life, death, and resurrection of Jesus of Nazareth.

I have often thought that, since God is God and does not change, we already know God's last judgment on us creatures. It is the same as God's first judgment, repeated over and over again in Genesis 1: God looked at the universe and saw that it was good. But because of the sacrament of God's love we have been given in Jesus Christ, this time we will believe it.

6. Spirituality and Eucharist

Rev. Kenan B. Osborne, O.F.M., Franciscan School of Theology, Graduate Theological Union, Berkeley, California

I. Eucharistic Spirituality Is Based on Community

The major theme of this essay is the following: Without a Christian community of some form, the celebration of Eucharist has no meaning at all. Eucharistic celebration and a Christian community are so intimately united that one without the other is meaningless.[1]

Consequently, an essay on eucharistic spirituality is also meaningful only on the basis of a eucharistic celebration and an underlying Christian community. There can be no discussion of eucharistic spirituality unless there is, first of all, a eucharistic celebration. Both the spirituality and the celebration, however, are unintelligible unless both exist within the reality of a Christian community. However, a major question arises regarding the kind of community needed to ground both the celebration of Eucharist and the development of a eucharistic spirituality. Throughout the many centuries of Church history, this question has engendered many answers, and even today the issue of this relationship is presented theologically in a variety of ways.

Before we focus directly on the several major answers to the question of this relationship, a factual situation should be noted. In

---

1. The validity of a eucharistic celebration does not depend only on the presence of a validly ordained priest who uses the correct matter (bread and wine) and who uses the correct words. To be valid, a eucharistic celebration must take place within a Christian community. The presence of a Christian community constitutes a basis for the valid celebration of any Eucharist. This essay does not attempt to prove this issue; such a proof is not the thesis of this article.

today's Roman Catholic parishes throughout the United States attendance at Sunday Mass has gone down considerably. In order to regain those not attending Mass, pastors and parish staffs have focused on remedial measures. Their primary remedial measure, in most cases, has been a focus on the quality of the eucharistic liturgy itself. In order to encourage parishioners to attend Mass, pastors and the parish staffs have generally centered their energies on improving the Sunday eucharistic liturgy. The choir is upgraded to a semi-professional status. The décor of the altar-area is enhanced by floral arrangements and artistic banners. A ministry of greeters is established to welcome people as they enter the church. Church bulletins are vastly improved through a professional-looking layout. Efforts to improve Sunday homilies are diligently made. Pastors and parish councils have exerted a great deal of energy to make the Sunday eucharistic liturgy a prayerful service which hopefully will draw more and more people to Sunday Mass. I am sure that all of us, in one way or another, have experienced a parish in which major efforts as described above have been made to enhance Sunday liturgy. This exertion of energy, expenditures of money and time, and the detailed planning of each Sunday's eucharistic celebration have had a single purpose: to improve the celebration of the eucharistic celebration so that more people will attend Sunday Mass.

Over the course of time, some of these parishes have run out of energy, and the Sunday liturgy has begun to take on a more mundane and formalized character. People notice this, and, as a result, the number of people at the Sunday celebration of the Mass begins once again to dwindle. A major question arises for all of this effort: What went wrong? The immediate answer is the following: The Sunday eucharistic liturgy itself has become humdrum and needs to be re-enlivened all over again. Pastors and parish councils have continually focused on liturgy as the central drawing point for the local church. Their intention is good, but the choice of liturgy as the starting point is the Achilles' heel which has helped but has not resolved the primary issues. The first focus, in my argument, should not be on the eucharistic celebration itself nor on the development of a eucharistic spirituality. Rather, I will argue that prior to any major expenditure of time and effort on an improved eucharistic liturgy or a deepened eucharistic spirituality, the development of a more profound Christian community must be the central reality of one's time, energy, and commitment.

The biblical theologian Jerome Murphy-O'Connor published an article some years ago which has continued to be influential: "Eucharist and Community in First Corinthians."[2] In his conclusion, Murphy-O'Connor writes:

> *The dominant characteristic of Paul's treatment of the Eucharist is its extreme realism. There is no exalted poetry, no flights into mysticism. It is firmly rooted in his concept of the community of faith as the basic reality of the New Age introduced by the death of Christ.*[3]

Murphy-O'Connor goes on to describe Paul's view of the community of faith: "Christ remains incarnationally present in and to the world through the community that is his body."[4] He continues, "The person of Christ is really present under the sacramental species only when the words of institution are spoken by 'Christ,' [namely] an authentic community animated by the creative saving love which alone enables humanity to 'live.'"[5]

That a community of faith, eucharistic celebration, and eucharistic spirituality are intertwined is not a new way of thinking. The *Catechism of the Catholic Church* echoes Murphy-O'Connor's

---

2. Jerome Murphy-O'Connor, "Eucharist and Community in First Corinthians," *Living Bread, Saving Cup* (Collegeville, MN: The Liturgical Press, 1982).

3. Ibid., 29.

4. Ibid., 30.

5. Ibid.

emphasis on Christ as the celebrant of a sacrament. The text of the *Catechism* answers the question posed in the very title of this part of the *Catechism*: "Who Celebrates?" The answer is stated succinctly: "Liturgy is an 'action' of the *whole Christ (Christus totus).*"[6] This same idea is repeated later: "It is the whole *community,* the Body of Christ united with its Head, that celebrates."[7] A community, *totus Christus,* celebrates the Church's eucharistic liturgy. The eucharistic liturgy is not celebrated simply by the priest. The Church is a community of faith, and consequently the eucharistic action is a community celebration dependent on the very existence of a Christian community. Only on the basis of this fundamental Christian community and its subsequent celebration of the eucharistic meal is there a possibility for a eucharistic spirituality. It is precisely this triadic relationship of spirituality, eucharistic celebration, and a community of faith that constitutes the heart of this essay.

The community of faith, however, can be defined in many ways, and in Church history the community of faith has appeared in many forms. Let us consider some of the major forms of this triadic interrelationship of eucharistic spirituality, eucharistic celebration, and eucharistic communities that have been evident in Roman Catholic Church history.

A. The Ideal Community of Faith

Perhaps it is best to begin with the ideal community of faith. Naturally, such an ideal community of faith has never existed. Nonetheless, the ideal has enlivened many efforts for the building of community, which one finds in our Church history. This ideal formulation is precisely what Paul in his First Letter to the Corinthians had in mind. In Corinth, Paul encountered the existential celebration of Eucharist by the Jesus community. Thus, the

---

6. *Catechism of the Catholic Church,* no. 1136. Italics and Latin are in the original text

7. *Catechism of the Catholic Church,* no. 1140. Italics are in the original text.

actual celebration of the Lord's Supper was, existentially, the point of departure.

Paul's reaction to this actual, existential eucharistic celebration in Corinth was negative and critical. In Paul's view, the celebration was deficient since there was no evidence of a solid and profound eucharistic Christian community. He, therefore, took the Corinthians to task not on the basis of their celebration of Eucharist, but on their lack of a credible Christian community.

Paul's focus on the community of faith is not simply an issue of interrelationality. Paul indicates, in no uncertain terms, that the Christian community of faith in the Corinthian gathering is the necessary and *sine qua non* reality. It is the foundation and basis for eucharistic celebration. Paul's complaint is primarily focused on their totally inadequate community of faith.

Only when there is an adequate community of faith can there be a true eucharistic celebration of the Lord's Supper, and only on the basis of these two can we speak of a eucharistic spirituality. The one area which causes the most divergence and becomes thereby the most problematic is the community of faith. What does "community of faith" signify? Paul, in his letter to the Corinthians, clearly specifies what an ideal community of faith entails. Murphy-O'Connor presents the following qualifications:

1. The Community Is One

The term "body of Christ" too often focuses on the different parts of a body and, by application, to various parts of the Christian Church. Murphy-O'Connor states that Paul focuses more on the organic unity of the body image. He states:

We think of individuals coming together to create community. For Paul it is precisely the reverse. The community is a radically new reality (1 Corinthians1:28) which makes the believer a new creation (2 Corinthians 5:17). We consider unity as something to be created, whereas Paul saw this unity as primary and envisaged individuals as being changed by absorption into that unity.[8]

2. The Community Is Christ

For Paul, the community is the "incarnational prolongation of the mission of the saving Christ. What he did in and for the world of his day through his physical presence, the community does in and for its world."[9] Murphy-O'Connor continues, "By entering the community, which is Christ, through faith and baptism, believers are absorbed into the organic unity which is 'one man.'"[10]

3. The Community Is Alive in Christ

If the community is what God intended it to be, then and only then are they alive in Christ. There is, however, sin in the community. A major aspect of a sinful community is disunity, and disunity means that a community is neither Christ nor alive in Christ. Paul goes on to indicate that sin is often brought about through the manipulation of the community by its leaders to act in ways that are contrary to the goal of living in Christ.

Structures, endorsed by the leadership, are most often the major areas of sinfulness in a community. It is not the individual who is the sinner and who thus compromises the community; rather, it is the community structure, endorsed and manipulated by the leadership and by the quiet acquiescence of others, that is the sinfulness of a community. Hostile divisions were taken for granted by the Corinthians; jealousy and strife became a habitual pattern of their life.

At this point we begin to perceive a basic reason for Paul's inexorable emphasis on community as the basis of all true Christian reality.

---

8. Murphy-O'Connor, "Eucharist and Community," 5.

9. Ibid., 6.

10. Ibid., 7.

> *Not only is it the mode of existence willed by the Creator, but it is the only practical concrete means whereby an individual is rescued from the false orientation of a fallen world. Only in an authentically Christian community is the individual free to be as God intended.*[11]

Freedom for men and women is not an individual thing. It is rather a quality of community that benefits others. Without a community committed to living Christian values, there is no genuine freedom.[12] In Corinth, the leadership of the Jesus community holds a Eucharist in which those who are wealthy eat well, while those who are poor are snubbed. There is no unity, no Christ as community, no life in Christ in such a eucharistic community. In such a eucharistic banquet there is structural sin manipulated by those who are important, and there is an absence of freedom in Christ.

This description is the ideal community which Paul proclaims; it is the ideal faith-community in which the Eucharist is genuinely celebrated and from which eucharistic spirituality emerges. Unfortunately, most Christian communities are not ideal, and, thus, there is in most Christian communities structural sin and a lack of freedom. Let us consider some of these "other" and non-ideal communities in which the Eucharist is and has been celebrated and in which some forms of eucharistic spirituality have emerged.

B. Trent to Vatican II: Priestly Eucharistic Spirituality

In the pre-Vatican II Church, when the Mass was in Latin, the priest or priests celebrated the Eucharist and contact or interaction with the lay people attending Mass was almost nil. Thus, there were two communities: the eucharistic priestly community and the eucharistic lay community. Let us consider, first, the eucharistic priestly community.

---

11. Ibid., 13.
12. Ibid.

Priests celebrated the Eucharist every day, often with only a few people present, sometimes with only an altar boy, and even sometimes with no other person present. There was indeed a eucharistic priestly celebration, but it was a celebration which was dominated by priests. Lay men and women were part of the celebration only in a peripheral way. There was indeed a eucharistic priestly celebration, but there was no community which included lay people. The community was theologized as a priestly community.

Priests celebrated the eucharistic liturgy in a language (Latin), which generally only they understood. Latin was foreign to the ordinary people. Priests had their backs turned to the lay people so that the people could not really see what was going on. In large churches, there was the chancel, an entire large section of the church between the altar itself and the lay people in which monks or canons had their places. In this setting, the lay people were even farther detached from the priest and the altar.

In this setting, there developed a very strong priestly eucharistic spirituality in which the lay people did not share. In the lengthy period of time from Trent down to Vatican II, many books were written on priestly eucharistic spirituality, and seminarians were trained to formulate their spirituality in a eucharistic way. Theology encouraged this by teaching that ordination separated priests from all other Christians because priests alone could change the bread and wine into the Body and Blood of Christ. Hence, there was this unique spiritual bond between the ordained priest and the Eucharist, since the Eucharist, theologically, was the key reality which constituted his priestly identity.

The spiritual and theological material of this period of time stressed the prayerful preparation needed for the heaven-shaking celebration of the Mass by a mere priest. The material also stressed the prayerful and meditative thanksgiving after Mass that the priest should follow in a serious way. The material stressed the purity needed for a priest to celebrate the Eucharist, and the emphasis was on the undeserved gift that a priest had received from Jesus to celebrate the eucharistic mystery.

Conclusion on Priestly Eucharistic Spirituality

From Trent to Vatican II there was a well-developed eucharistic spirituality, but it was a spirituality only for priests. The eucharistic priestly spirituality was grounded in a faith community, but again the faith community was the faith community only of priests. With the development of the seminary system following Trent, spirituality of priests became a major focus and this contributed greatly to the positive reformation of the Church itself.[13] Such a eucharistic spirituality, however, is short-sighted, since it does not reflect the entire Christian community of faith. Priestly eucharistic spirituality without lay eucharistic spirituality can only be seen as an underdeveloped eucharistic spirituality. This leads to the next theme: the eucharistic spirituality of the lay person from Trent to Vatican II.

C. Trent to Vatican II: Lay Eucharistic Spirituality

From the Council of Trent to the Second Vatican Council, the ordinary lay woman and man in the Roman Catholic Church attended Mass, and thus the Eucharist was a major part of their spirituality. In contrast to the priestly eucharistic spirituality, the lay eucharistic spirituality during this period of Roman Catholic history took on a different form. We can explain this lay eucharistic spirituality as follows. First of all, there is the eucharistic lay celebration in which the lay person is basically an onlooker. Secondly, since no eucharistic celebration takes place without a spiritual community, there was indeed a eucharistic spirituality, but it moved in the direction of devotion rather than a spirituality based on central theological positions regarding the sacrament of the Eucharist itself. We have,

---

13. See K. Osborne, "Priestly Formation: The Council of Trent and the Second Vatican Council," *Trent and Vatican II: Change and Renewal,* ed. Raymond Bulman and Frederick Parella (Oxford: Oxford University Press, 2005).

therefore, a eucharistic celebration but with a distinct spirituality, namely, a eucharistic devotional spirituality.

The key word in this phrase is "devotional." Without participation in the eucharistic celebration itself—a participation which was clearly reserved to the priest—the lay people were considered onlookers with only a minimal amount of participation. In fact, their main liturgical participation was receiving the Eucharist, but they received communion *from the hands of a priest.* For the rest of the Mass, the lay people were generally on their own. Being on their own, they developed their own spirituality. Many good lay men and women recited the rosary during the Mass. Others read from their devotional prayer books—which for the most part were not missals. Only in the 1940s, 50s and early 60s did some people follow the Mass itself in English (or another vernacular language) while the priest alone celebrated Mass in Latin. Here again, the participation was simply following in English what the priest actually was doing at the altar.

An excellent reference for this form of spirituality in the United States can be found in *Prayer and Practice in the American Catholic Community* written and compiled by Angelyn Dries and Joseph Chinnici.[14] In this volume one finds documentary evidence of such devotion between the years 1785 and 1979. It indicates, with textual verification, how lay men and women throughout those years developed a spirituality, in many ways eucharistic, but not at all the same as a theologically endorsed eucharistic spirituality.

During these centuries a eucharistic spirituality for lay men and women did indeed develop, so that the "onlooker" situation of lay people did not lack a eucharistic spirituality. As a result, there was a community of Catholic lay men and lay women who were devoted to the Eucharist and who, thus, formed a eucharistic community.

---

14. See Joseph P. Chinnici and Angelyn Dries, ed., *Prayer and Practice in the American Catholic Community.* American Catholic Identities Series (Maryknoll, NY: Orbis Books, 2000).

As noted earlier, during the period leading up to Vatican II, American Catholics attended Mass, but during Mass they focused on their own devotions such as the rosary, other prayers in their own language, or in the 1940s, when English missalettes became popular, simply reading along while the priest performed the eucharistic liturgy. This devotional eucharistic spirituality certainly enriched many lay women and men, and the Mass provided a special time to nourish this devotional eucharistic spirituality. However, the Mass alone was not the energizing source for this devotional eucharistic spirituality. There were also such prayerful moments as visiting the Blessed Sacrament, Benediction of the Blessed Sacrament, and the processions for Corpus Christi.

Not all eucharistic devotions and forms of spirituality during this lengthy period of time can be considered the best way to celebrate the Eucharist. St. Paul would have had a great deal to say negatively about Benediction, private visits to the Blessed Sacrament, and the Corpus Christi processions. The focus of his critique would be that the center of such spirituality is devotion not the actual eucharistic celebration which we call the Mass. We see this in three distinct forms:

1. In many instances, even today, the chapel in which the Blessed Sacrament is reserved is far more elaborately decorated than the altar itself. There are many more flowers on the ledge in front of the tabernacle than on the main altar of the church. There are more candles burning in front of the tabernacle than on the altar in the church itself. In other words, the visual décor for the tabernacle upstages the visual décor of the main altar in the church. To rephrase the famous remark of Queen Victoria, St. Paul would not be amused.

2. On Holy Thursday there is the procession to the so-called altar of repose. However, in many churches and chapels the altar of repose is decorated in an elegant manner, and people come to

spend an hour or so at the altar of repose. Once again, the décor of the altar of repose often surpass the décor of any celebration of the Eucharist in the main part of the church with perhaps the exception of Christmas. St. Paul would not be amused.

3. On the feast of Corpus Christi, there were traditionally elaborate processions, with benediction given in three different places, all of which had altars richly decorated with flowers, banners, pictures, and incense. St. Paul would not be amused.

Conclusion on Lay Eucharistic Spirituality

The forms which lay eucharistic spirituality took during the centuries from Trent to Vatican II were indeed eucharistic spiritualities, but they were all devotional spiritualities. By this, I mean they were focused on private devotion more than on the actual celebration of the Lord's Supper. The community of faith was present in the many lay men and women, and their faith was genuine. However, their faith was more personal than communal, more prayer-centered—that is, on devotional prayers—than Eucharist-centered, and more non-sacramental than sacramental. Such a eucharistic spirituality, in spite of all its good points, does not truly measure up to the ideal eucharistic spirituality as described above in which the three entities (spirituality, eucharistic celebration, and a community of faith) form an integrating whole.

Efforts today to combine both priestly and lay eucharistic spiritualities into a meaningful unity are clearly evident. The deficiencies of both the priestly and lay eucharistic spiritualities are clearly seen, and the efforts to combine the two are rightly praised. However there are some problematic situations. Let us focus on these problems. This is the second part of my presentation.

II. Eucharistic Spirituality: The Highest Spirituality

A contemporary third form of eucharistic spirituality has developed in the Roman Catholic Church and it has been based theologically on certain texts from the documents of Vatican II. In these conciliar statements we hear that the Church reaches its pinnacle of being Church in the celebration of the eucharist.

In the Vatican II document, *Christus Dominus*, the Decree on the Pastoral Office of Bishops in the Church, we read:

> *In carrying out their work of sanctification, parish priests should ensure that the celebration of the eucharistic sacrifice is the center and culmination of the entire life of the Christian community.*[15]

In *Lumen Gentium*, the Dogmatic Constitution on the Church, we read:

> *Taking part in the eucharistic sacrifice, the source and summit of the Christian life, they [the people of God] offer the divine victim to God and themselves along with him.*[16]

In *Presbyterorum Ordinis*, the Decree on the Ministry and Life of Priests, we read:

> *In the most blessed eucharist is contained the entire spiritual wealth of the Church, namely Christ himself our Pasch. ... The Eucharist appears as the source and the summit of all preaching of the Gospel....Therefore the eucharistic celebration is the center of the assembly of the faithful over which the priest presides.*[17]

---

15. *Christus Dominus* (Decree on the Pastoral Office of the Bishops in the Church), no. 30.

16. *Lumen Gentium* (Dogmatic Constitution on the Church), no. 11.

This same positioning of the Eucharist as the source and summit of ecclesial life is found in the *Catechism of the Catholic Church*, nos. 1324-1327. In this section, the *Catechism* cites *Eucharisticum mysterium*, an instruction sent to the entire Church by the Congregation of Rites which states that the Eucharist "is the culmination both of God's action sanctifying the world in Christ and of the worship men offer to Christ and through him to the Father in the Holy Spirit."[18] The *Catechism* concludes this section by stating, "In brief, the Eucharist is the sum and summary of our faith...."[19] These words are theologically and spiritually puzzling. A sacrament is the sum and summary of our faith? What about God, what about the Trinity, what about the Incarnation?

Two major issues arise which demand a better hearing and explanation by Roman Catholic theologians and leaders:

1. Is the presence of Jesus on the altar, which takes place during the eucharistic prayer, more important than the proclamation of the word of God, which takes during the first part of the eucharistic celebration?

2. Can the Eucharist of the altar be theologically and spiritually understood without also understanding the Eucharist of the world?

These two questions, both theologically and spiritually, need much more discernment and study than we find in contemporary literature on the sacrament of the Eucharist. Let us consider each of these issues.

---

17. *Presbyterorum ordinis* (Decree on the Ministry and Life of Priests), no. 5.

18. *Catechism of the Catholic Church*, no. 1136; *Eucharisticum mysterium*, no. 6.

19. *Catechism of the Catholic Church*, no 1327.

A. The Eucharist and Its Relationship to the Word of God

The Eucharist, that is the celebration at Mass which involves the consecration of the bread and wine into the Body and Blood of Christ, is referred to as the apex of the eucharistic liturgy. Nonetheless, the reading of the word of God, which was in the past called "Mass of the Catechumens," is officially today seen as integral to eucharistic service. In *Sacrosanctum Concilium*, the Constitution on the Sacred Liturgy, we read:

> *The two parts which in a sense go to make up the Mass, that is, the liturgy of the word and the eucharistic liturgy, are so closely connected with each other that they form but one single act of worship. Accordingly, this sacred synod strongly urges pastors of souls that, when instructing the faithful, they take care to teach them to take part in the entire Mass, especially on Sundays and holy days of obligation.*[20]

In the same conciliar document we hear that the celebration of the Eucharist is the principal manifestation of the Church.[21] In *Lumen Gentium* we are told that the bishops, above all in the Eucharist which they themselves offer, manifest the fullness of the Church.[22] At times, mention is made of the word of God in connection with the Eucharist, but most often the Eucharist is presented as the renewal of the sacrifice of Jesus, the paschal mystery, or the offering of bread and wine. Although the bishops at Vatican II clearly stressed a deeper appreciation of the word of God, the Vatican II bishops, just as the Roman Catholic bishops who preceded them, have never addressed the central role of the word of God, which the churches of the Reformation stressed in such a profound way. The Roman Catholic

---

20. *Sacrosanctum Concilium* (Constitution on the Sacred Liturgy), no.56.

21. *Ibid.*, no. 41.

22. *Lumen Gentium* (Dogmatic Constitution on the Church), no. 26.

Church is the true Church because of the four marks: one, holy, catholic, and apostolic. Even in the explanation of these four marks, the veracity of the Roman Catholic Church is most clearly argued, stated, and described through the mark of apostolicity. In contrast to this ecclesiology, the churches of the Reformation stress their own validity as true church by means of the word of God which is the foundation and essence of any and every true Christian church. For these churches, spirituality develops from hearing the word of God and living it. Spirituality might be eucharistic, but it is above all a spirituality based on God's own word.

Although the bishops at Vatican II stressed the reading of the word of God for all sacramental celebrations, the reading of the word of God can be omitted in the sacraments of reconciliation and anointing of the sick, and the reading of the word of God is ancillary in the new rubrics for baptism and confirmation. Even for the Eucharist, the first part of the "integral" liturgy is not totally integrated. To miss the first part of the Mass is not perceived as contrary to obligation in the same way as missing the second part of the Mass, the eucharistic prayer.

For Christian spirituality, the word of God is central. Many saints reflected in solitude on the word of God. In doing this, they were apart from all other people, within the confines of their own living quarters, or outside in an eremitical place—that is, on a mountain, by a lake, and so on. In meditation, these saints were caught up in the unitive way. The peak of their spiritual journey took place not at a eucharistic celebration but at a time when they were deeply meditating on gospel life.

There is much work that needs to be done by theologians, spiritual writers, and Church leadership vis-à-vis the relationship of Roman Catholic spirituality and the word of God. Eucharistic spirituality alone is not the entire dimension of gospel spirituality.

B. The Eucharist of the World and the Eucharist of the Altar

The Eucharist is a meal, in which we celebrate the communion of people eating together. They are eating the fruit of the earth and the work of human hands. They are tasting the spiritual depths of the mystical body of Jesus. Too often, as people leave the church, they leave the Eucharist. Theologians, such as Juan Segundo and Karl Rahner, have raised a question about the Eucharist of the world. Already in the thirteenth century, the Franciscan theologian St. Bonaventure spoke about the three books which every Christian in his or her journey to God must read each day: the book of creation, the book of the gospels, and the book of one's own personal experience. A full spirituality takes into account the book which the Creator God spreads before us each day in the various worlds we live in. All things have been made by this loving God, and, therefore, we find brothers and sisters far beyond the Church, and we find sacraments far beyond the seven. If we miss seeing God in our fellow men and women, if we miss seeing God in the world about us, how can we say with any surety that we really do see God, but only in the confines of the Roman Catholic Church? God, the Creator of all, is not limited to the Church. If we do not read and meditate on the gospels, the word of God, we will miss what God, the loving parent, is saying to us. God speaks beyond the sacraments, although God speaks there as well. In a place of major importance for all Christians, God speaks to us in the word of God, proclaimed to us by others, and meditated on by us in moments of private prayer. The word of God is foundational for Christian spirituality and cannot be set to one side through an overemphasis of the seven sacraments. Finally, in the world we experience, there are moments of unitive contemplation, given to us through God's loving grace. *Gaudium et Spes* states this reality very clearly:

> *Deep within their consciences men and women discover a law which they have not laid upon themselves and which they must*

*obey. Its voice, ever calling them to love and to do what is good
and to avoid evil, tells them inwardly at the right moment: do
this, shun that. For they have in their hearts a law inscribed
by God....Their conscience is people's most secret core, and
their sanctuary. There they are alone with God whose voice
echoes in their depths.*[23]

In this profound depth of one's own being, where we are alone with
the Holy Spirit, we are reading the book of our own spiritual experience, the third book, which cannot be read alone, but must be
read together with the book of the world and the book of the gospels.

Eucharistic spirituality is an important focus, but in developing
that focus we must continually go back to the three books: the created world, the gospels, and one's personal experience. Eucharist
nourishes, and the life we lead is a life in this same created world
which also gives us life and to which we also give life. It is led, for
Christians, within a gospel framework, and we must let the Gospel,
the word of God, speak to us. This Gospel is written in the Sacred
Scriptures, but we preach the Gospel and, therefore, hear the Gospel, and sometimes it is preached and heard through words. More
often than not, we preach and hear the Gospel in a wordless way.
Eucharistic spirituality is a personal spirituality as well as a communal spirituality. God speaks to us alone in the depths of our heart
and conscience. Our heart or our conscience, then, is a third book
on spirituality, and just as the Eucharist is internalized into our bodies, so too is it internalized into our own hearts. There, in our personal depths, God becomes one with us—the unitive way—and we
become one with God. Being one with God is the primary goal of
all spirituality. Sacramental Eucharist is part of spirituality, but

---

23. *Gaudium et Spes* (Pastoral Constitution on the Church in the Modern World), no.
16.

spirituality reaches deep into the Eucharist of the world and into the Eucharist of our heart and conscience.

Care on this issue, however, is in order. Edward Kilmartin, in his essay "Theology of the Sacraments: Towards a New Understanding of the Chief Rites of the Church of Jesus Christ," speaks about the sacramental understanding of all reality.[24] Even more strikingly and more recently, Louis-Marie Chauvet, in his volume *Sacrament: A Sacramental Reinterpretation of Christian Existence*, states that "Creation is itself charged with sacramentality."[25] In chapter three, however, Chauvet makes a better and more carefully constructed sentence, for he says that the world is a possible sacrament: "Le 'profane' du monde et de l'histoire est ainsi reconnu comme le lieu sacramental possible d'une histoire sainte." ("The 'profane' of the world and of history is also recognized as the possible sacramental location of a sacred history."[26])

The universe, the world, or our human history is not automatically sacramental. Rather, it is a sacramental possibility. In other words, it can be or become sacramental. This is a better way of speaking. Bonaventure did indeed speak of the exemplarity of God in all creation, but he did not say that this presence of God in all creation was evident to everyone indiscriminately. Alongside the exemplarism of Bonaventure is his illuminationism, which is God's gifting to us the ability to see God's presence in the world at large and in our hearts. Without this illumination, our eyes, minds, and hearts are blinded.

---

24. Edward Kilmartin, "Theology of the Sacraments: Toward a New Understanding of the Chief Rites of the Church of Jesus Christ," in *Alternative Futures for Worship, General Introduction*, v. I, ed. Regis Duffy (Collegeville, MN: The Liturgical Press, 1987), 123-175, esp. 157-161.

25. Louis Marie Chauvet, *Symbole et Sacrement: Une relecture sacramentelle de l'existence chrétienne* (Paris: Les Éditions du Cerf, 1987). English trans. P. Madigan and M. Beaumont, *Symbol and Sacrament: A Sacramental Reinterpretation of Christian Existence* (Collegeville, MN: The Liturgical Press, 1995), 551.

26. Ibid., 565.

Still, one can say that the world is sacramental, or more sharply, possibly sacramental, if we might open our eyes, minds, and hearts to the grace of God. In other words, in creation, including the depths of our conscience, God is present. When we see God and wherever we see God, we are faced with the true sum and summary of our faith, and God is greater and superior to any and every sacramental celebration of God's presence, no matter what kind of celebration this might be.

III. Conclusions

All of the above should speak volumes to lay women and lay men. The book of creation is not a priestly book; the book of the gospels is not a priestly book; the book of one's experience is not a priestly book. We are first and foremost human beings, and these are all human books. We are also Christians, and from our Christian stand-point, we can be nourished by these three books. We are ecclesial, sacramental and eucharistic, but we are also part of the book of creation itself in which all things can be sacraments of God's real presence. We live day-by-day as we listen to the word of God, and we spend moments of aloneness in our heart. In and through all of this, God can be united to us and we to God. This is the unitive way, and this unitive way is the goal of all spirituality.

In the Eucharist of the world we come face to face with a creating God. St. Bonaventure compares God's presence to the impression that a ring gives to the wax which seals the letter. On the wax is the seal of the prince, the king, or another important person. However, Bonaventure goes further. One can remove the ring from the surface of the wax, and the design of the ring remains on the surface of the wax. For Bonaventure, it is better to imagine all creation as the surface of water. One can place his or her ring on top of this surface, and just as it was in the wax, so too the image of the ring makes an impression on the surface of the water. However, when one removes the ring from the water, the impression is gone. In creation, which is more like the water than the wax, God is present and his presence is impressed on each and all created realities. Take God away and the creature disappears as well.

One could say that in the intellectual and theological tradition of the Franciscan Community we are not *created* by God. Rather, we are *loved* into existence by God. We are not only loved into existence by God, we are loved in an absolutely free way into existence by God. Creation also can connote that God makes something and then leaves it alone. Love, on the other hand, freely cherishes someone or something into existence, which remains in being only as long as God lovingly cherishes it.

For the Franciscan tradition, the Incarnation in many ways is conjoined to creation itself. Both—Creation and Incarnation—form the most important real presence of God and of Jesus. The real presence of Jesus, in this tradition, makes no sense whatsoever unless it is seen as one manifestation of an even deeper and broader real presence: the real presence of God in the created and incarnational universe. It is in this created and incarnational universe that we experience the Eucharist of the world, and in turn the Eucharist of the world helps us understand the Eucharist of the altar.

Panel Discussion

Richard Miller: The first question is for all the speakers. Is spirituality internal, external, personal, social? Which are essential to it?

Michael Himes: I'll start off. The answer is yes. This was stated so wonderfully by Colleen Griffith, and then was echoed by Mike Buckley, and, in fact, was able to be heard in various ways in all of the talks. Spirituality embraces every dimension of the human being. All of the ways we relate to one another and ultimately all the ways in which we relate to God are embraced under the heading of spirituality. We exist as individuals, but we also exist as members of communities. We have personal, inner lives, but we also have external lives—lives lived in company and in public with others, and all of those are dimensions of our spirituality. Indeed a person who thought that one of those dimensions was exempted from their spiritual life would be living a very unhealthy spirituality, I think.

Michael Buckley: I would agree with that very much. I would like to add one thing. Spirituality is not only this kind of pattern of relationships that Michael Himes describes: both internal and external and so forth. But it is also the reflection upon spirituality. There is a discipline now of spirituality, which Sandra Schneiders has celebrated in her work, that is really important for the Church in the United States and for religious orders to look into seriously. It's an evaluative, descriptive, phenomenological study of what is the experience of people in various spiritualities. So, I would just like to add that there's spirituality then as a practice, as a pattern, and there's spirituality as a discipline.

Richard Miller: This is also a question for the whole panel. What is the role of apologetics in spirituality and religion today? You might want to define apologetics.

Michael Buckley: I would say that one of the faults of apologetics of the sixteenth century was the excision of spirituality as part of the self-manifestation of the reality of God in Christianity. Look at books that were written in the fifteenth or sixteenth centuries—Mansen is a good example, Canisius is another. When they came to the reality of God, they proved God by so many proofs—Thomas Aquinas' *Quinque Viae* is an example—the digging up of ancient proofs that one would find in the theological discourse of Cicero and so forth. What they didn't do is they didn't bring out the manifestation of holiness in the lives of the saints or the narratives of holiness or the practices of holiness, and the result was that they talked about God like the way they might have talked about the planet Pluto. That you could prove by the perturbations on Neptune that there was a planet Pluto and so forth. Just so you could prove there's a God because of the nature of the contingent universe. But it all died because people would not long believe in a God that you don't communicate with. And no matter what kind of abstract, inferential proofs you had, what spirituality offered was some sort of direct interpersonal relationship with God—"direct" being understood in many different ways. And when you took that out, you were saying, without actually saying it, that the religious lines of spirituality have no cognitive value. They really cannot in some way aid or buttress or in some way strengthen apologetics, and I think that was a disaster. I've argued elsewhere that that is one of the principal causes of the rise of atheism in the western world.

Mary Ann Hinsdale: This is not an area of my expertise, but it intrigues me. I do know enough to know that there's a sort of resurgence particularly in the areas of religious education and formation in faith, to teach apologetics and to offer courses in apologetics. What interests me is "why"? Where's this coming from? A couple things occur to me. First, there's probably—I've experienced this myself as a teacher—a lot of concern and dissatisfaction about the degree to which we have solid formation in faith as Catholics, whether we're talking about our children or adolescents or ourselves as adults. The question, however, is "What is the best way to go about remedying that situation."? And we could have a whole other workshop actually, or a whole day, talking about that, but what I am brought up short by, when I go to these Web sites and I take a look at some of the materials, is—and we were talking a lot about this today—the almost total absence of mystery and the tendency towards idolatry. To have the ready answers, pat, sure—which really goes against the theme I was concentrating on, which was to reflect on what does it mean to be created, as a human being; that we need to be aware of incompleteness, our finitude.

So, to the degree that apologetics gives us a false security—that we have the answers now; therefore, we can defend our faith—I'm not against that, but I think there are other ways to go about it. I am also thinking back to the second century apologists and that word and what it comes from etymologically, which is a very important thing, which is basically to be able to listen to a culture and utilize the symbols, language, and realities of a culture to then bring the Gospel into play using the words, and methodologies, and symbols of the particular culture. I am talking about what we have learned from missiology: basically what is called enculturation or interculturation actually today because we always have to remember too that the Gospel itself grew up and is expressed in a particular culture. So, we have to take that kind of a need for interpreting what the Gospel is actually saying as well as listening to the culture about how best to express it, so there's a kind of dialectical relationship. I just haven't found personally that apologetics is necessarily the right approach to remedy the disease we have with our level of maturity

in terms of faith if it's simply ready-made answers that stop thinking and stop the appreciation of mystery.

John Strynkowski: I'm reminded of Karl Barth's statement that the
best apologetics is good dogmatics. So, we could paraphrase that
and maybe say that the best apologetics is also lived spirituality, as
Michael Buckley was saying, and my suspicion is that fifty years from
now, Thomas Merton will still be on the bookshelves of Barnes and
Noble and the current apologists will be forgotten.

Richard Miller: This question is for Father Strynkowski. What does
it mean to search for meaning, and can the search for meaning cause
oversimplification of the Trinity? That is, to reduce it down to my
understanding?

John Strynkowski: Well, I think I'll answer the second part first. I
think that I, as an individual, a member of the Church, would always have to be attentive to the entire tradition so that I don't engage in a reductionism or I don't narrow down the Trinity to my
perceptions of it. So, I would always have to be studying, or be attentive to, the entire tradition, to the experience of the Christian
community. The search for meaning is part of what it means to be
human, but people can settle for meanings that don't make them
authentically human. They can settle for meanings that are maybe
in some ways idols, or they don't want to enter into relationships
that are meaningful. So, I don't think we can escape the search for
meaning, but the danger is to settle for meanings that are less than
humanizing.

Colleen Griffith: I'd like to jump in here. Somehow I think we ought
to be less concerned about reducing the Trinity to our own individual perceptions of the Trinity and more concerned with opening
up the Trinity. I don't now how many of you were taught Trinity in

school using the famous shamrock on the board. I remember sisters in school who, during Trinity week, would put the shamrock on the board and say, "It's like this: three in one. Once you have that down, it's a mystery, and we're done. We're done because it's mystery, and that's about all we can say. But here we have an example in the shamrock of the three in one. Do you get it?" And that would be a lesson on the Trinity. I think that rather than leading with fear, we ought to lead with desire to open up this great mystery. One of the contemporary accents in theology these days is Trinity. We've had some wonderful theologians, women and men, reminding us that—this is going to be theological, technical language—the economic Trinity is the imminent Trinity and the imminent Trinity is the economic Trinity. In other words, whatever we say about God with respect to who God is within God's self—if you want to know what that looks like or what that is, look at God's salvific ways toward us. And all of the ways in which God is toward us are in fact truly who God is. There's not some sort of special remainder over here, some secret element within God that we never enter. God's giving of God's self presumes this full giving. When we unite that imminent and economic Trinity, then it has all kinds of repercussions for our lived faith, for our spiritualities. We ought to want to know what we're doing when we say "In the name of the Father and of the Son and of the Holy Spirit" or "Glory be to the Father, and to the Son, and to the Holy Spirit." Many of us were taught these prayers, and that was it. We know how to recite them, and we know them well. They're recognizable, but what are we really saying about God's ways in terms of those "persons"? When we talk about our desire for union with God, are we recognizing that desire as a desire for union with those ways of God? Are we recognizing that this living God is inviting us into these particular activities? Then the Trinity opens up. I think that rather than starting with fear, with respect to an approach, following our own best desire to know God more deeply in this threesome way is a good thing.

Richard Miller: This is a question for the whole panel. It's a question about the dynamic of doctrines or the development of doctrine. Doctrine versus dynamic or complete set of given truths. Do we understand doctrine as a complete set of the truths, or is there development? This seems to be a matter of intense debate now: When is discussion on doctrinal questions officially closed?

Michael Himes: In the beatific vision. That's when it's closed. When you see God face-to-face, the issue is closed. Until then, the issue is open. Seriously, remember God does not give us creeds. God does not give us doctrines. God does not give us information. God does not give us commandments. God gives us God, and for 2000 years in the Christian tradition and for thousands of years before and around the Christian tradition, we have been trying to explore, unpack, live out that experience, that self-giving of God. The ultimate self-giving of God, the unique, the unsurpassable self-communication of God is the Incarnation, God's gift of God's self in the life, death, and destiny of Jesus of Nazareth. But we're still unpacking that. We're still learning that. And there's no point at which we can say, "Well, we've got that right, one hundred percent." This is why we notice the Church's way most often in its history of defining a doctrine is to define it negatively. This can sound somewhat forbidding, but it really is not designed to be. It was simply because we knew we couldn't say it positively. "Let anyone who says thus and so be an *anathema*." You see, that was not simply condemning heresy; that was saying we know these limits. If you go that way we know you are wrong. If you go this way, we know you are wrong. But in between here, we don't know what to say. We can tell you what we're sure is inadequate, but we can't tell you with finality and with certitude and with completely finished exactness what is right because we are still exploring the mystery. It is still being lived out. There are certainly definite stages of doctrine, in the development of doctrine, but it's only complete when we reach the beatific vision.

Kenan Osborne: The question that you have here is in many ways a really good question for today. I'd like to put it this way. When Jesus was preaching and teaching, he used Aramaic and he was talking in Aramaic to Semitic and Jewish people. After the resurrection, as the early followers of Jesus began to think about this, you have the gospels and the writings of Paul, but these are all written in Greek. So you already have a beginning of an intercultural blending, of taking what Jesus said and putting it within a Greek format which already changed the earliest meaning a little bit. We can't say that that's what you're going to end up with. Then, as we moved into the end of the second century and more people were Greek-speaking and came out of the Greek culture and less people came out of the Jewish world, this entire Greek philosophy began to take over. Middle Platonism and Plotinus and things like that, and a lot of our dogmas were thought out during that time and were expressed in Greek and come through a Greek culture.

Then we had, beginning around 700 or 800 this immigration from Bulgaria and places beyond Bulgaria that they call the German migrations. So these would be the Burgundians and the Goths and the Ostrogoths. A new culture came in, and there was a second enculturation issue, and we see that basically in cannon law and in liturgy. But after that time, even with Aristotle coming in (that was still Greek), there really wasn't another enculturation. But what we have today is a third major enculturation movement in our Roman Catholic Church with the Church for the first time having various dialogues with non-Christian religions, whether they are African or Asian or native South or North American kinds of religions. This is going to change what we would mean in a question like: What is dogma? Because we always speak of a dogma as something that has already been said and is wrapped up. But if you would take the concept of there being two natures in the one person of Jesus and try to put that into Chinese, it's not going to come out the same. Or if you put it into Vietnamese or into Korean, it's not going to come out the same. Now that's what's going to be happening within the next almost fifty-to-a-hundred years with the enculturation process—and a development of dogma, if we have to say it at least linguistically, which changes the mentality too, is going to take place for the next hundred years.

John Strynkowski: I am reminded of something Basil the Great wrote about. It was at a time when there was still a lack of clarity regarding the Holy Spirit. He had concluded a homily by saying, "To the glory of the Father, with the Son and the Holy Spirit." Some people complained and said that he was making the Holy Spirit equal to the Father and the Son. Of course they couldn't write to Rome because there was no one to write to in Rome at that point. So he defended himself by saying, "I didn't invent this formula. This is what I have heard from the faithful in the cities and in the countryside." So, as long as there are faithful, wherever, there's going to be development.

Michael Buckley: This is a very difficult and delicate matter because we have so screwed up the essential role of the Church in teaching doctrine by insisting upon practices and statements that the vast majority of Catholic people have not accepted. So, you're living in a unique position now, a position of some violence, theologically speaking, because, for the first time in an awful long time in the history of the Church that I can recall, you have the non-reception of official teaching by the faithful, and these two parallel lines go on, and I don't know where it's going to go. But let me say a word very much in favor of the dogma. There is no physical, there is no linguistic formula that is ever going to be adequate to the mystery of God. Secondly, the purpose that the Church has in defining, and I agree with Michael 100 percent, is not to clarify the mystery; it's to keep the mystery. If you want to explain why Jesus Christ was so successful at what he did, you cannot explain that by saying he was God pretending to be a human being or a human being pretending to be God. Neither of those will wash. How do you get together man and God and so fourth? I don't know how you get it together. That's a function for theologians, but you've got them together because that's the reality that is there. It is the mystery, and the Church has the obligation of not only keeping it, but also the obligation to preach and teach it. It's going to use formulations to do so; you simply have to. Words crackle, they give out, but you have got to use them. And worse in terms of burden, they have to ask for faith in what they say. That God so loved the world that he sent his only begotten Son. Now, why do you accept that? Because father or the bishop or the lay instructor is intelligent and probative? If you build everything on that, you build it very much upon a kind of human faith, and the more clever man or the better argument wins out.

So, if there is not some sort of presence of God to his Church inhibiting the imposition upon the faithful—that is, clergy and laity—of that which is positively erroneous, then there is no right the Church has to ask for faith in what it says. If there is not some sort of divine presence within the Church keeping the Church from positive errors along those lines and serious errors along those lines, I don't see how you could actually do the basic work of the Church in terms of preaching and teaching. For centuries the Church had a way of differentiating those things which were matters of faith— and those were quite rare—from those which were the common teaching of the Church, which is *doctrina catholica,* which was ordinary, or the stuff that was kind of certain and a lot of people held it and a lot of people didn't hold it, and so forth. We had a way of doing it; we don't have it now. And the difficulty of not having something like the theological notes is that everything now has become part of a level plane. And that everything from the presence of Christ in the Eucharist to women can't be ordained to birth control to the infallibility of the pope; all those kinds of things are now meshed together in one potpourri that does little other than cause confusion.

Richard Miller: This next question is for the whole panel and dove-tails with Father Buckley's response. Can you have an authentic Catholic spirituality which at the same time does not accept some of the teachings of the Church?

Mary Ann Hinsdale: I think Father Buckley answered this question, actually. There are gradations of teaching. Dogma and doctrine, for example, are not the same. We don't have a list of the dogmas. The best you can do is the creeds, but you can pay attention to the for-mulations. Ecumenical councils have a greater degree of authority than the pope's angelus address at noon on Sunday at the Vatican. These are not all of equal value, so you would really have to know what you are talking about. But once again, and these are principles of ecclesiology, infallibility of the Church refers to our assurance that the Holy Spirit will not leave us so high and dry that we'll be in the boat on our way totally off the beam—basically not be respond-ing to God and believing what God has revealed to us. But for some-thing to be infallible, there needs to have been a consultation that this is, in fact, the faith of the whole Church. Now we don't have mechanisms for that in ways that other churches do; it's kind of a felt sense. Bishops, the shepherds, really need to know the flock; theo-logians need to be consulted, theologians of a variety of schools. There's always been pluralism in theology, and I don't remember all the principles of hermeneutics of dogmatic statements at this point, but you can go back and read, interestingly enough, Avery Dulles, who back in the 80s wrote a little book called *The Survival of Dogma*. I was just looking at it recently, and he outlines there very important principles with regard to consultation of what the faith of the people is, consultation of theologians, taking a look at the different formu-lations used for various Church pronouncements. It makes a differ-ence if something was defined at an ecumenical council, or if it was in a papal encyclical, or if it was a document from one of the Roman congregations, or a pastoral letter of a particular bishop. These are not all of the same degree or weight. That doesn't mean they are not authoritative in their own contexts, but they are certainly not all infallible. Again it's this leveling of the field that you spoke about, that I think brings up that question.

Kenan Osborne: It's a very interesting question because you use the word "authentic," and as you probably know, authentic comes from a Greek phrase. It's a wonderful word because the Greek word means "yourself," "I myself." To be authentic means to have a good grasp on yourself, that there's integrity about who you are. We're not very authentic when every fad comes and we just follow the crowd. That's non-authenticity. And so there's integrity that comes in: Can I be an authentic Christian? If you want to say Christian, you are not just talking about yourself, you are talking about a community. So you have to experience that there is an integrity about what your stance is with the people who make up your community. A Christian does not want to be inauthentic. In the past, there have been very authentic Catholic people who were true to themselves and their communities and resisted pressures to be inauthentic, Francis of Assisi being one of them and Clare of Assisi being one, a woman. When the pope came and stayed overnight with Clare and her sisters—I think she gave him some nice wine or something like that—she got him to sign something that he had not wanted to sign, but for her own community and for the integrity of how she put the Gospel together. This was what she wanted. And that integrity is what makes us a good Catholic or a good Christian. It isn't that we have something out here; the integrity is in asking others "Can I say this and still be authentically good?" When they say it sounds like it is OK, I'm being helped along. Authenticity doesn't mean that everything that comes out from the authority is accepted just as it is because there are times when we have to be critical about the way the Church might be acting. This "authentic" is a wonderful word. That you have yourself and you have control of yourself, and therefore there's an integration there.

Michael Buckley: I agree with everything that has been said. I would just give a footnote of something for the present confusion. I am speaking about the infallibility of the pope. There are probably seven times in the history of the Church, a period of approximately 2000 years, that the pope has spoken in such a way as to demand a response to an infallible teaching. All of those were subsequently approved by a council, with the exception of the two Marian doctrines. I believe that's correct. I think Newman was quite right. I have no problem dealing with the infallibility of the pope. I think it's true. I think in those very rare circumstances it can be exercised, but it simply is not that big of a deal. We have used it so rarely in the history of the Church, and now because it's so forefront in the people's consciousness, they think that everything that is said is either infallible or it's nonsense. This is terrible. I don't know how we're going to come out of this situation, but the confusion of the teaching authority and function of the Church is one of the paramount dangers to the contemporary Church.

Richard Miller: This question probably goes to the issue of authenticity as well. In the contemporary context that Dr. Griffith spoke of, it seems like a cosmic soup consisting of these differing and competing spiritualities. How do we see those? Are we passing a negative judgment? How do we deal with that? It's not so clear as to what to make of the present context.

Colleen Griffith: That is a great question. I certainly, in my opening comments, did not intend to pass judgment on specific practices, but rather to call into question for us some of the capitalist strategies of making commodities of some very rich, for example, Asian traditions. Take the practice of yoga, a watered-down version of yoga in our pastoral institute. I hear about some of our graduate students taking these hot yoga classes. This is the new rage. I don't know if any of you are familiar with hot yoga, but you do these yoga classes, and you sweat profusely because the temperature is so very high. They are doing it because it's a great way to get trim and it's a great way to lose weight. Now somehow I don't think that is holding the breath of what yoga means within the great eastern religious traditions. So there are certain things I think we need to be suspicious of here.

However, when we're talking about putting spirituality and doctrine back together, it never precludes learning from other traditions. We continue to learn from other traditions as we do within our own tradition. If you've ever had the occasion to be a member of an interreligious dialogue group, people will often say that when they heard of a practice that was significantly "other"—coming from another tradition—that it caused something to rise up in them by way of the reclaiming of something they hadn't thought about in a long time in their own tradition. Something like the practice of yoga, for a woman coming back into her own tradition, perhaps gives her new eyes for looking at statements regarding the body, the kind of theology of the body that might be found in her own Christian tradition. It may cause us to find things that we never realized were in our religious tradition. Dominic's nine ways of prayer, for example, which highlights lots of gestures and postures that are possible for prayer, or something like *The Way of the Pilgrim,* which is an Eastern Orthodox classic regarding the power of prayer that is not just verbal, but drops down into prayer of the heart and is really a felt bodily prayer that's tied to the breath. One begins to find all kinds of things within one's own tradition having been exposed to a practice in another tradition and having begun to wonder about the possibilities within one's own religious traditions.

Richard Miller: This is for the panel as well. It follows the preceding question. In what ways can Christian spirituality advance the work of interreligious dialogue?

Kenan Osborne: Spirituality is certainly one of the major issues within interreligious dialogue today. You sit down at a table with Buddhists, Taoists, and Catholics from the western hemisphere, and we want to take it through the intellectual sphere, and that isn't really the way they understand things, so they all say "Why don't we all go and pray together or something like that or meditate?" or "Why don't we do something different and just sit around and talk more in a doctrinal, metaphysical kind of situation?" I don't think there's been a good way of figuring out how interreligious dialogue is going to work out. But there is this growing understanding that if they don't see in one another something of holiness, then no matter what you say, it really doesn't carry any meaning. It's sort of an unwritten presupposition that if we don't see you in the holiness, including working with the poor, then we don't see you as authentic. So in a Federation of Asian Bishops Conferences, if they don't see a dialogue with the poor, and therefore the justice issue and its implications, then the authenticity isn't there. It's a big thing. That's an area in which you can't say, "Well, how is spirituality working out in there?" You take your shoes off when you go into a Buddhist temple. I think what we should be doing is taking our shoes off when we're face-to-face with other religions as a sign of reverence. The reverence simply means this is something that I feel is holy. I may not understand it, but by taking my shoes off a few times, I begin to understand that there is something holy there.

Richard Miller: This question is for Father Himes and Father Osborne. If everything is a sacrament, does this water down our Christian spirituality?

Michael Himes: It waters it up! What you've just done is to take the notion of sacramentality and removed it from seven special rituals which are preformed by certain communities on special occasions. You said that you're living in a world that is just floating, soaking, yes, dripping in grace from top to bottom, that there's never a moment that you get away from grace, that there's never a point at which you're outside of grace, and that, in fact, if you're not graced you're not damned either—you simply don't exist. Everything that exists does so because it's graced. Now, Father Osborne, very wonderfully, I think, said it exactly right: Not everything is sacrament, everything is a potential sacrament. What makes it sacrament is when somebody notices it. That's when it becomes sacrament. Gerard Manley Hopkins was quoted, I think, twice in the course of the day. I'll give him a third run. In "*Hurrahing in Harvest*," a poem that you may well know because it's one of his most frequently anthologized poems, Hopkins speaks about the fact that he's teaching at a boys' school in Wales, winter is coming on, and he's not looking forward to winter. If you've ever experienced winter in Wales, you'd know why. The fog lifts just enough so you can see the mud. Suddenly he finds himself saying, well, wait a moment, check out the foliage turning at this time of year, the fall. Think of the way the clouds come by, think of the joy of the harvesters bringing in the harvest. The next to last line, the ultimate line in the poem is, "These things, these things were here, but the beholder wanting." The leaves didn't change color at that moment, the harvest didn't begin at that moment; it was already going on. What changed was Hopkins. Hopkins hadn't noticed it; now he did. What was missing was someone to notice it and to be a beholder. That is, in my opinion, the single most beautiful expression of the sacramental principle in the English language. These things were here, but the beholder was wanting. It is saying that, in fact, grace is omnipresent. Grace is theological shorthand for talking about why there are things instead of there not being anything. It's because grace, the self-communication of God, lies at the root of everything. The only reason everything exists is because God loves it and God gives God's self to it absolutely. To see anything for what it is, to see it as God sees it, is to see it as absolutely rooted in love. What can be perceived that way? Absolutely everything. What are needed are people to notice it. The whole of our ritual sacramental celebration, the celebration of the seven communal sacraments, is an enormous training in becoming sacramental beholders. That's what it's about. It's a huge training. If you can see that the water that's poured on this child's head is the giving of grace, then you can discover that the water you use to make tea this morning and the water in which you take a shower is also grace. If you can recognize that this little bit of bread and this little bit of wine becomes the fullness of the presence of God in Christ, then you can recognize that the bread you had last night with friends and the wine you shared over the pasta, is also, at least possibly, at least capable of being transformed into the fullness and the presence of God in Christ. One realizes that there is nothing that exists which is not graced; and all is seen as graced, perceived as graced. There is nothing that cannot be an occasion for the communication of grace to us. The whole thing is sacramental from beginning to end, from top to bottom. The thing is just dripping with grace. It's all about grace.

Kenan Osborne: When you have documents from whatever source saying something about sacraments—even my own books on sacraments—they are all *about* sacraments. The only time you have a sacrament is when it happens. It's a happening. It's a very existential situation. If I were to get up now and stand there and say, "I'm a sacrament! I'm a sacrament!" Richard Miller would come very cautiously over and say "of what?" and "for whom?" We just don't go out and say this is sacrament and that is a sacrament, but at a certain moment, the "of what?" and "for whom?" comes together. When you go into an art museum you walk around. You stand here, you stand there. You get in one place where the light is just right and you suddenly see what that picture is all about. And that's what happens existentially to us. We've been to many celebrations of the Eucharist. Are they all sacraments? I don't know, but some days they speak.

And that's what we need: a sacrament that speaks to someone of something. It's there, but you can't read it. In Kaufmann's introduction to his book on the basic writings of Nietzsche, he says you don't read Nietzsche for what he's saying to you. You're looking over his shoulder, and he's pointing, "Do you see what I see?" And you say, "No I don't." Look again, and you'll see what he sees. Similarly, that's when a sacrament is a sacrament.

Richard Miller: This question is for Sister Hinsdale. Why do you think obedience has taken a bum rap today? What does obedience mean in the light of our creaturehood touched by both the infinite and finite?

Mary Ann Hinsdale: Obedience. I need to have a better understanding of what is meant by obedience, and in what context, and why it would have a bum rap. If we're thinking of post-modern pluralism—the attitude of "I do what I feel like doing and what I want to do, and I'm the authority unto myself"—that's possibly part of the attitude that no one has the right to expect obedience from anywhere else. The question was something about the finite and the infinite, but I didn't quite get what was asked.

Richard Miller: Maybe the issue is how do we understand obedience and what's the proper way of understanding obedience and spirituality.

Michael Himes: I think a very dangerous and destructive understanding of obedience—which is a virtue—is the submission of one person's will to the will of another. That's not obedience; that's slavery. That's a very different thing. Nobody ever said slavery was a virtue. Obedience is a virtue. Nobody in the Church is ever asked to take a vow of slavery. People are asked to take vows of obedience. Obedience is not the submission of one person's will to the will of another. Obedience is fidelity to reality. Obedience is the point at which you recognize that this is the situation, this is what's needed, this is what you have to offer, and you respond accordingly. Obedience is not when the bishop tells you do X and you go out and do X. Obedience is when you find yourself in a situation in which clearly what is needed is X. Nobody else is around to do X except you. You thought it would be nice to do Y. Nobody's interested in Y, and nobody needs Y, but they need X. And you say, "Well, I guess I'll do X." That's obedience. It's fidelity to the truth of circumstances, but it is certainly not slavery. It is not the submission of one will to another. That's gotten a very bad rap in our time and richly deserves it.

Mary Ann Hinsdale: I just thought of something else. When I hear the word "obedience", I think of being asked to answer a call, responding to a summons in a certain sense. Think of Teresa of Avila, for example, or any of us, for that matter, who feel some sort of call, perhaps in the context of our relationship with God. This is where I experience my finitude and resistance. I find myself saying or feeling, "Not yet; I'm not quite ready to do *that*, to respond to that call." So there's often a struggle with obedience in this sense. Again, I take comfort in those wisdom figures who spend many years saying "no" or "not yet" until finally, because of the relationship that they have with God, they can pray or ask, "Help me respond." It's something that we cannot do alone. Again, if everything is grace, including our own response, we cannot do this unless we are given it. So there's a nice kind of tension there, but also something I find very consoling. God doesn't demand the impossible of us. I'm firmly convinced of that. What God does demand or ask, God will give the grace for us to respond. That's what the question evoked in me.

Richard Miller: This is for Father Osborne. I'm going to give you three questions. I'm going to let you sort it out. If the community is not in unity, how can the Eucharist be truly celebrated? Given the seemingly increasing polarity between conservative and liberal religious doctrine, how does spirituality play into that divisiveness? What do you do to build Christian communities?

Kenan Osborne: Pastorally speaking, before you try to answer how you "make" any sacrament meaningful, maybe your parish or community needs to be encouraged to take a year to think on what it takes to build up a reconciling community or a compassionate community for those who are ill and sick—a year in which we want to see eucharistic people in their homes, eucharistic people in their dealings with their husband or wife, with their children, with their grandparents, with their parents. Let's try to see what a believing community is before we ask why you came and joined us in our faith. I think that's what I was trying to say. The focus of our effort should not be in trying to make the liturgical or sacramental celebration something that is attractive and wonderful unless we've already laid some foundations of being a reconciling community. In other words, we need to see the Eucharist in each other and having a community of faith before we let five more people enroll in the RCIA. I think we need to do that first. I think that's what Paul was saying. He knew the Corinthians weren't going to be perfectly united, but he was telling them, to their leadership particularly, that they needed to develop a more unified kind of community in which the word of God really means something, where the word of the Gospel really does mean something, and the message of Jesus really does mean something. And then let's talk about how we can celebrate these days, times, and places that you mentioned. That's how I would want to answer all three.

Appendix I

A Sampling of Written Questions Presented at the Symposium

I. Questions for Dr. Colleen M. Griffith

1. Are you proposing that all the popular spiritual practices you mentioned are inherently bad, negative, nonproductive or anti-Christian? (After many years away from the Church, one of the things that brought me closer to God is what I learned in yoga philosophy and practice in meditation. Though I don't subscribe to all of the philosophy in the yoga tradition, I do feel that it has made me more open to coming back to the Church and relearning the teachings of Vatican II. I do practice yoga and I'm very deeply connected to my Catholic roots and my adult relationship with Jesus Christ and his Church.)

2. Are we discussing today, the subject of spirituality, because we dare to, when what we really want or need is to examine the subject of religion but we dare not, at least not openly in the presence of the hierarchy?

3. Can you see any value or progress in moving those who are "only" seeking spirituality into doctrinal spirituality?

4. If Catholic doctrine asserts that women are intrinsically incapable of sacramental ministry, how can women connect their spirituality with or be enriched by such a doctrine and its Church or religion?

5. If I claim to be spiritual and not religious, is it the same as claiming I am a good person but religion does not matter because I will still go to heaven since I believe in God?

6. Is spirituality internal? external? personal? social? Which are essential to it?

7. What do you see as the benefits/weaknesses of a focus on "apologetics" in relationship to spirituality and religion, especially with regards to religious education at all levels?

8. How can we integrate more modern spirituality into our parishes without damaging doctrine?

9. How do you see gender, economics, and race affecting spirituality and religion?

10. Is doctrine dynamic or static, a complete set of given truths? This seems to be a matter of intense debate now. When is discussion on a doctrinal question officially closed? What is the difference between doctrine and dogma?

11. How can the Church do a better job of integrating doctrine and spirituality for the young?

12. Please give a specific example of what might connect a doctrine of Roman Catholicism and human spirituality, e.g., for a catechist on an RCIA team.

13. These words and concepts are wonderful. But how do we affirm the common person in their everyday spirituality?

II. Questions for Msgr. John J. Strynkowski

1. From pre-Vatican II through Benedict XVI, what are our traditions as in "Spirituality is informed by our tradition"?

2. You said the Catholic Church seems to be less involved in social affairs. Could it be that society wants it to be less involved because its problems have caused the Church to be a less of an authority for Christian teachings?

3. Are you familiar with the Holy Spirit as Sophia? Could you comment on this in spirituality, especially for women?

4. If heaven is not a "place" and is in each one of us, what happens when we die? Or when someone we love dies?

5. If God is both everywhere and nowhere, where am I going when I die (presuming I am going where God is)?

6. How would you relate your image of the triune God within the human person to our traditional way of looking at the Father who sends Jesus into the world, Jesus who leads us back to the Father through the mutual gift of the Spirit?

7. Can the search for meaning cause over-simplification of the Trinity?

8. What does it mean to "search for meaning"?

9. If the Holy Spirit fuels our search, when do we know we have found what God wants us to search for?

10. Did humanity know of the triune God prior to the Incarnation?

11. Our "search for meaning" presumes a certain freedom from certain basic needs: (food, shelter, freedom from fear). Where do you see Jesus' quest for meaning?

12. How is the "desert experience" so critical to Trinitarian spirituality and how can we who minister foster and provide such experiences for those to whom we minister?

III. Questions for Rev. Michael J. Buckley, S.J.

1. Would you comment more on the incarnational, spiritual dimension of the Eucharist as a continuing "physical" presence of God in our life?
2. What do you think the present Pope's spirituality is: ascent or descent? How do you think his spirituality will influence the Church?
3. You speak of Christ's descent into history and life and the Christian's discovery of Christ in the ordinary. Please specify practices and movements elicited by that discovery. In other words, what do we do with this discovery?
4. Is it appropriate to attempt to combine incarnational and ascending spiritualities?
5. What are the differences of conscious awareness in Ignatian and Buddhist Spirituality?
6. Which emphasis, ascent or incarnation spirituality, will serve the Church better in the near future, particularly in its U.S. context?
7. Given Matthew, chapter 25—what might be called the Christian believer's "final exam"—is it fair to say that an "ascent" spirituality is insufficient if it doesn't ultimately lead to an incarnational spirituality?
8. Talk about what salvation means to you without using evangelical terms.
9. Would you say ascent spirituality and descent spirituality offer equal opportunity to expand one's personal spirituality?
10. How do theologians image "salvation," "Kingdom of God," and "Kingdom of Heaven"?

IV. Questions for Sr. Mary Ann Hinsdale, I.H.M.

1. You mentioned the turbulence and stress in our everyday lives, caused by or directed toward other people. How do you handle these stresses?
2. Given the conservative climate in our Church today, what do you see as the role of women? And what could be women's response?
3. Why has "obedience" taken a bum rap today? What does obedience mean in the light of our creatureliness, touched by both the infinite and the finite?

4. In view of your thoughts on the gender issue of God, how are we created male and female in the image of God?

5. How do we as Catholics incorporate our own experience of God into our perception and inclusion of our Muslim brothers and sisters as God's creatures?

6. Do you think that the notion of "Natural Law," which has been so prominent in our theological thought, still holds the same validity today?

V. Questions for Rev. Michael J. Himes

1. When Jesus said "My Father in me always hears me" does that mean the Father/Mother in *me* always hears me is also true?

2. How did human beings, not God, change?

3. How do we reconcile your view of the abundance of God's grace (that is always present) with talking about searching or discerning God, given the notion of the ascent tradition in spirituality?

4. As I read Jesus' stories, forgiveness always comes before repentance or asking for forgiveness. Please comment.

5. How do you respond to the thoughts of some people who say that we live in a culture of death, instead of seeing the world as graced?

6. If God is not changed in salvation but we are, what do we need to do to be saved? Do we need to ask for salvation? Or do we need to *realize* our situation?

7. Sr. Hinsdale talked about insisting on the maleness of God borders on gender idolatry. As an enlightened man, can you help other men in this audience understand how the exclusive maleness of God affects women's spiritual lives or women's spirituality?

8. How does the sacrament of reconciliation fit in with the approach you have suggested to our understanding of God's forgiveness expressed in the parable of the Prodigal Son?

VI. Questions for Rev. Kenan B. Osborne, O.F.M.

1. In what ways can Christian Spirituality advance the work of interreligious dialogues?

2. Is everything a sacrament? How does this not "water down" Christian spirituality?

3. If the community is not in unity, how can Eucharist be celebrated with integrity?

VII. General Questions

1. Can homosexual persons living in a relationship have an authentic Catholic spirituality?

2. Why is the hierarchy trying so hard these days to distinguish clergy from laity when community, coming together in Christ, is the essence of Church?

3. Is Satan—the devil—a figure of spirituality rather than of doctrine, properly speaking? Is there a useful role for the devil in contemporary belief or spirituality?

4. As a practicing Catholic, when someone says, "You're religious, I'm spiritual," how do I answer?

5. We find more young adults who seem to be more conservative and rigid. What have we missed in teaching them and being role models for good spirituality (i.e., relationship with God and community)?

6. Many flee organized Christian religion because they don't see the religious doctrines informing us about our relationship with the planet. If religion doesn't give us good information and wisdom about that relationship, the human race has a dim prospect for a future. What can be done about this?

7. Living in a diocese that for years embraced the spirituality of Vatican II's *Gaudium et Spes*, but now is pushed toward "restoration" and what feels like regression, how does one nurture and keep alive a healthy spirituality?

8. I am impressed with the speakers. They all seem to be on the same page. I wonder why the hierarchy of the Church isn't listening to them. Are they fearful of this way of thinking or do they think we are being heretical?

9. What is the role of apologetics in spirituality and religion today?

10. Can you have an authentic Catholic spirituality while at the same time not accepting some of the teachings of the Church?

11. What is more important to have: a good spiritual life or a good religious life?

12. What can we do to purify our image of God?

13. How do we reconcile the fact that John of the Cross says as we get closer to God we become more unique with the emphasis on community? Is there as great a danger in an escape from one's self in community as there is to making spirituality simply a private affair?

14. Given the seemingly increasing polarity between "conservative" and "liberal" religious doctrine, how does spirituality play into that divisiveness?

15. If my own spirituality is at odds with Church teaching in some areas (e.g., teachings relating to sexuality, the death penalty, etc.), what steps could you illustrate to reconfigure my spirituality to conform to the Church's teaching?

Appendix II

Speakers' Biographies

Dr. Colleen M. Griffith

Colleen M. Griffith has a doctorate in theology from Harvard Divinity School. She is faculty director of Spirituality Studies at the Institute of Religious Education and Pastoral Ministry, Boston College, and directs the Advanced Certificate in Formative Spirituality. Dr. Griffith also directs retreats and provides spiritual direction.

Msgr. John J. Strynkowski

Msgr. Strynkowski is a priest of the diocese of Brooklyn who received his doctorate in sacred theology of the Pontifical Gregorian University, Rome. He has taught in seminaries in the U.S. and in Rome. Msgr. Strynkowski served at the U. S. Conference of Catholic Bishops in the office of Education for Catholic Higher Education and as Executive Director of the Secretariat for the bishops' committees on Doctrine and Pastoral Practices.

Rev. Michael J. Buckley, S.J.

Father Buckley is Professor of Theology at Boston College. Among his numerous and influential articles and books, he has written on the subject of *Papal Primacy and the Episcopate: Towards a Relational Understanding.* For three years he was executive director of the U.S. Catholic Bishop's Committees on Doctrine and Pastoral Research and Practices. Father Buckley served as President of the C.T.S.A., recipient of their prestigious John Courtney Murray Award, and most recently as the Director of the Jesuit Institute at Boston College.

Sr. Mary Ann Hinsdale, I.H.M.

Sr. Mary Ann Hinsdale is a member of the Servants of the Immaculate Heart of Mary and Associate Professor of Theology at Boston College. Her doctoral dissertation topic was on Hans Küng's use of Scripture. She has served as secretary to the Catholic Theological Society of America and vice-president of the Catholic Theological Society.

Rev. Michael J. Himes

Fr. Michael J. Himes is Professor of Theology at Boston College. Fr. Himes teaches courses and has received the Phi Beta Kappa Award for Outstanding Teaching. While a professor at the University of Notre Dame, he was twice voted Most Influential Teacher by graduating classes. The many people in many parish halls around the country who have used his videotapes in their adult faith formation classes will attest to his influence on them as a teacher also.

Rev. Kenan B. Osborne, O.F.M.

Fr. Osborne, a Franciscan priest and Professor of Systematic Theology, *Emeritus,* at the Franciscan School of Theology in Berkeley, California, is a scholar, writer, and teacher. Father Osborne has mentored hundreds of scholars through their masters' degrees and doctoral studies preparing them for Church service. He has served his religious community in leadership both nationally and internationally, written twelve books, and led major Catholic theological organizations.